Futurescaping

Futurescaping

Using Business Insight to Plan Your Life

Tamar Kasriel

BLOOMSBURY
LONDON · NEW DELHI · NEW YORK · SYDNEY

First published in the United Kingdom in 2012 by

Bloomsbury Publishing Plc
50 Bedford Square
London WC1B 3DP
www.bloomsbury.com

A CIP record for this book is available from the British Library.

ISBN: 9-781-4081-5664-3

This book is produced using paper that is made from wood grown in
managed, sustainable forests. It is natural, renewable and recyclable.
The logging and manufacturing processes conform to the
environmental regulations of the country of origin.

—

Design by Fiona Pike, Pike Design, Winchester
Typeset by Saxon Graphics Ltd, Derby
Printed in the United Kingdom by Clays

To Vishal
& Harry
& my family

CONTENTS

Acknowledgements

Firstly I would like to thank Amanda Munilla for all her assistance. I am very grateful too to all the people who were willing to come in to test the futurescapng methodology for their time and openness. I would like to thank as well all those who have been so generous with their advice and wisdom: Wendell Bell, Nina Castell, Richard Cleeve, Polly Courtney, Kevin Duncan, Rodney Fitch, Sylvie Gagnot, Andy Gilbert, Alan Giles, Katerina Gould, Lucinda Hallan, Jennifer Hamilton, Daniel Khaneman, Mike Roberts, Philipp Rode, Carole Rosati, David Rosenberg, Lauren Zander. Thanks also to Lisa Carden for her enthusiasm and encouragement.

Finally, I would like to thank my sisters, Daphne and Emily, my mother and stepfather, Judith and Willy Margulies, and Vishal. For everything.

Introduction

'Where do you see yourself in five years' time?' That dreaded interview question, for which whatever they tell you, you know there actually *is* a right answer. You want the job so you try to play it right – far-sighted but down to earth, proactive but not so ambitious that the interviewer feels threatened. Interview done, you leave your badge at reception and your focus zooms back in to tomorrow/next week/next month when you will or won't get the job, and the nearest relaxing drink.

It's a shame that this question rarely makes an appearance outside interviews. Very few people plan their lives. Planning is what you do at work, when there are other people to answer to, deadlines and bottom lines. Life is just too unpredictable and unwieldy to manage like a business. And surely life is what happens *to* you, and planning will take out the excitement and romance, right?

Well, not necessarily. Just because you've thought about the future doesn't mean events are going to play out any differently, that the mystery is gone. Rather, it just means that whatever turns out, you'll be a bit better prepared, better rehearsed, better able to see and, maybe, seize an opportunity. With so much possibility and uncertainty out there, we need to impose the frameworks to help us navigate the unknown.

Why futurescaping?

How do you imagine the future? An open page? A thread going forwards from where you are now? A blur?

1   Attributed to Bruce Mau.

One of the triggers to writing this book was an eye-opening coffee with a close friend (the meeting was eye-opening, the coffee was mediocre). Outwardly successful, he had been leading a company effectively for some time: it had doubled in size every year for the last three years, attracted inward investment and powerful and smart people onto the board, yet it became apparent – as he crumbled his muffin into even smaller bits, describing his personal financial mess – that he was unable, or unwilling, to plan his own life beyond the next month. It just didn't make sense, that this corporate triumph should be so short-sighted. How could his work/life planning balance have gotten so unstuck?

When you think about it, it's amazing how many people who are extremely successful at work seem to suspend their critical planning faculties when it comes to their personal lives. What happens when they leave the office? Why do we put so much less effort into the things which are actually so much more important to us? As the Nobel prize winner Professor Daniel Kahneman summed it up when I interviewed him for this book: 'Most of what we do is ignore the future. We commit ourselves to a certain path that we have fallen into. Most people assume it will be like this, and just muddle through...People don't like rationality, especially when it matters.'

Researching this book, as well as talking to business leaders, behavioural economists and academics, I also interviewed several life and executive coaches in order to better understand some of the psychology behind planning, or the lack of it. All of the ones I spoke to had decided to turn their expertise to helping other professionals better manage and plan their careers, having done very well in their own. Despite divergent views across some topics, it was notable how much consensus there was on the strange way otherwise smart and accountable people can completely lose the plot when it comes to their own future.

Is there something we can do to get people to inject more rationality into personal planning? I'm hoping so. Why shouldn't we be able to take some of the essence of all that smartness, objectivity, accountability and creativity which we use at work to make our personal lives a bit more grounded, to add a bit of strategic thinking to how we run our lives?

Futurescaping aims to outline the benefits of future planning in the life of an individual and to show you how this can be usefully put into practice. It is a way of thinking which has been central to my professional life and, consequently, I believe it has practical implications when applied to the personal. It is different from both typical self-help and business books and instead brings together ideas from both genres.

I spotted a gap in the market for a sensible guide to planning for your individual future. My experience with Futureal, a consultancy which helps companies successfully deal with uncertainty and plan for their future, suggested there might be a way to fill the gap. Specifically, helping individuals build a model for their future, showing them how to keep a smart, watching brief on the outside world and how to identify relevant changes and frame a logical model to combine them, just as we do for business.

Corporate value

Since the economic crash of 2008, the corporate world has been under renewed scrutiny and attack. However, in amongst the blame, culpability and dirty corporate linen, there remains utility and ways of working which allow businesses to be highly functional and deliver products or services to (largely) satisfied customers. What can we, as individuals, learn from them? Well, along with the discipline enforced by objectivity and accountability, there is a raft of skills which companies use, including planning, and within that the particular technique of scenario planning, which can be borrowed or modified to become extremely useful for the individual.

Companies can take transformative decisions because they have particular skills and techniques when they operate commercially, that, in general, individuals don't. Most people barely analyze how transformational decisions will add value to their life. Business schools don't teach case studies of people. We don't have a system, a process to evaluate sensibly where a choice could take us. However, if only we could borrow some techniques from the boardroom, we can evaluate the pros (and the cons) of any transformational decisions that we might have the power to make, and be better prepared for anything the future might throw at us. How is a company able to make these transformational decisions? By having a rational framework. By being forced to articulate, to consider the costs and the potential long-term benefits, emotion can be defined and even marshalled.

As individuals, we are confronted with options today which will affect our lives for years ahead. The social and cultural changes of the past century mean that now, more than ever before, people are faced with a new and almost limitless range of possibilities in their lives. For example not just who to marry, but whether to marry at all. (Did you know in the US you can get wedding insurance? Firemen's Fund will insure you in case the venue burns down or if the groom's father has a heart attack. Wedsure will even insure against cold feet[2].)

---

2   'Wedding Insurance Protects Against Incidents On That Magical Day', Forbes.com, 20 April 2011.

What can individuals learn from how companies make decisions today, decisions which must make sense and profit in the future, to help them make smarter personal choices? Businesses understand that they don't operate in a vacuum. Decisions about strategy are made against a backdrop of external change and the broader environment. Similarly, as individuals, we all operate within systems of interconnected forces and we need to take account of them if we are going to make smarter decisions.

Self-help books tend to be very internally focused, but our private lives are also shaped by external factors such as economic crashes, the social changes and expectations around relationships, and environmental issues like climate change. While many people see these externals as unconnected and irrelevant to their everyday lives, they can have a powerful impact. So even if you were able to alter your outlook, behaviour, language or whatever the 'guru' recommends without taking into account the external factors, you are still largely an unwitting victim of chance – albeit a more spiritually enlightened one. While it might not seem like the most obvious factor determining a relationship, might an oil price rise, for example, increase the price of travel to the point where it becomes too expensive for a couple living apart to visit each other?

Rational rehearsal

This book draws on fifteen years' experience in analysing consumer behaviour for businesses and working with scores of successful organisations ranging from Fortune 500 companies to religious orders thousands of years old. It aims to show individuals how using the best bits of the corporate model, following a logical, rational process for decision-making and future planning, allows people to be more objective with their own lives and can help individuals free themselves from entrenched assumptions and thinking patterns. It will show readers how every area of their personal lives – job, family, relationships, finance, health, retirement – can benefit from a bit of thoughtful planning and 'rehearsal'. It will help them isolate which elements are within and outside of their control, and will allow them to appreciate that there is a range of possible future scenarios for how their lives could pan out, and how they might best frame, and aim for, the more desirable outcome.

In a world of ambiguity and flux, the future is uncertain and not predetermined. Farsighted companies understand the breadth of influence on their future and their decisions. People should too. On a human level, we have a surprising capacity to derail ourselves. We are not good at accommodating data, combining complexity or calculating risk. Nor is this something which all companies are good at. Those that aren't may manage to bumble along, but not for long before they die or get swallowed up by a smarter, or at least bigger, entity (think of Kodak, Cadburys...) We will leave them be. Rather, we want to turn our attention to companies which can do future planning well and from which we can learn because they are accountable and objective. That is the bit we want to borrow.

This thoughtful focus on the future is challenging because it requires dealing with uncertainty and some level of complexity. It is worth the struggle, though, because your life and your decisions are affected so broadly. It is about knowing your place in a wider world, aiming for objectivity. This book outlines a process that has all these things built into it. You don't have to do it all from A to Z straight off, but even if it simply makes you a bit more open to confronting and embracing uncertainty, and growing a sense of awareness about the complexity of the forces shaping your life, then you will be facing the future more smartly and better prepared than you were before.

When is the right time?

Any time can be the right time for future planning – unless the Mayans were right, there will always be a future[3]. These techniques are especially useful in recession. Previously, with cheap credit on seemingly limitless supply, it was possible for people to make almost risk-free decisions. Now the crunch means future options are more significantly impacted in a shorter time frame because you can't just put your mistakes on the not-yet-maxed-out credit card and move on. Just as companies are dealing with the fallout of rapid change and an uncertain future, there is more of a demand than ever before on us as individuals to be innovative and resourceful and to manage our lives thoughtfully. It is not an easy journey. When companies do futures work, the initial stages are often uneasy – it is far easier to ignore future possibility and threat than to face it. However, thinking rationally about the future leads to new clarity and new confidence, as unknown unknowns are diminished and more avenues open up.

Invented here

The future may be uncertain, but it is real. The most powerful way to get you to face and plan your future is not by trying to sell you a ready-made solution, but by giving you a process for addressing it.

---

3   There is some controversy, though, about exactly what the Mayans were on about. As reported by Reuters, according to Erik Velasquez – who, as etchings specialist at the National Autonomous University of Mexico, must surely know better than anyone – the theory that the Mayans predicted the world would end in December 2012 is just a 'marketing fallacy'. I'm with Erik.

Futurescaping includes the following chapters to help you make that process your own.

'Future Philosophy' considers the way different people and cultures imagine the future and how uncertainty is managed (or ignored). It looks at the role of utopias and development of self-help against the backdrop of social change. In order to future plan, we must be willing to accept that the future is not perfectly predetermined but rather is shaped by both our actions and external factors.

'How Companies Plan' closely examines the methods of corporations whose work and investments require them to look far into the future. These examples illuminate future planning and begin to suggest how this can be transposed from the professional to the personal.

'Human Drivers' examines the factors which motivate our decisions. From the simplest choices to the most complex conundrums, these 'drivers' influence each and every decision we make. This chapter helps you to understand which drivers might apply to your decision and which is the most fundamental.

'External Factors' shows you how to bring the outside in, discussing those issues which will impact your decision but are not personal to you or shaped by your actions. These are the 'uncontrollables': external factors which include everything from the economic climate to popular tastes. People often neglect to think about these factors which may have significant impact on the outcome of their decisions. While these cannot always be perfectly predicted, they can to some extent be prepared for and considered.

'Getting Objective' explains the importance of distance and detachment when making life planning decisions. You may be reading this book is because you are struggling to make an important choice. This chapter should help to clear the emotional haze which is surrounding your issue and let you picture your problem without a smoke-screen. Objectivity is key, not just to making a decision, but making the *right* choice which you won't regret.

'Combining Complexity' considers the ways in which we must account for a variety of factors when making decisions: especially in the case of long-term decisions, a mix of complex internal and external factors collides and coincides.

'Futurescaping', the key chapter in the book, outlines the process of scenario planning and shows how it might apply to individuals. Through a series of case studies and diagrams, this chapter gives a detailed explanation of the uses and way in which we can plan for the future. Remember: this process cannot make the decision for you. However, it will allow you to foresee the likely outcomes of your decision. Through this process, the idle musings and confused thought processes stimulated by wondering 'what if...?' are transformed into ordered, rational thoughts.

'Driving Back from the Future and Early Warnings' shows you how the results of future planning can help individuals and businesses illuminate the opportunities and barriers they face in long-term planning, and how to build a strategy and an early warning system so you are ready for whatever the future may bring.

1

Your Future Quotient

'Somedays even my lucky rocketship underpants don't help.'[4]

As you will see in Chapter 3, strategic planning for corporations is serious business. Trying to thrive in a world rife with uncertainty, they want to leave as little as possible to chance and so plan carefully and look ahead to determine likely and preferable versions of the future. This should be true for many individuals too – but it isn't. Top performers in business also realise that even the most careful planning won't allow you to avoid all unexpected chances, and therefore flexibility and responsiveness are also key. This is even truer for individuals. For example, a change in management may put a 'secure' job quickly in jeopardy. A sudden change in health of a family member may cause you to have to re-prioritise your time completely.

At Futureal, we have developed a system for evaluating how future-ready organisations are so we can evaluate their Future Quotient (FQ). It's useful because there's little point in spending money on fabulous new insight techniques if all the organisation wants to do is put their collective heads down and just stick to the knitting. Becoming future-ready is something which can take a bit of work, so you need to prepare to be prepared. We look at how open an organisation is to looking outside, how often and how broadly it looks beyond the immediate company concerns, and

---

how these external signals are interpreted and internalised. We assess how they see the future, what time frames they plan for, how frequently and fluidly they adjust their future model, and how they use these models to build strategy. We feed it through a simple model and hey presto, their FQ score emerges. A high FQ means a highly future-literate company, one that is well placed to withstand future shocks and well rehearsed when disruption comes. If we see a low FQ score, we realise that maybe it ain't broke now, but we need to get ready to do a bit of fixing.

Many of the FQ elements also make sense for individuals. For people, there's an added element of objectivity required which businesses take for granted. Some people may be better than others at being future-ready, at having a high Future Quotient, but all of us can improve our FQ. Wendell Bell, Professor Emeritus of Sociology at Yale, has been teaching the art and science of futurism for many years. As he describes it, 'I try to teach people that they can indeed have the power of many types of future knowledge through grounded predictions: if you're flying off an aircraft carrier, for example, when you head back you want to fly to where the carrier will be when you get there, rather than where it is when you start. A simple intercept problem. To take another example, Wayne Gretzky has said, 'A good hockey player plays where the puck is. A great hockey player plays where the puck is going to be.'[5]

This book is unlikely to teach you to be a good ice hockey player or land on an aircraft carrier, but it will show you how you can really get the most out of your life by being future-ready. But how, exactly, do you start this thinking process that many are too overwhelmed to do? How do you know if this book is for you? (It

5   In conversation with the author.

is, it is). The first step is to evaluate your Future Quotient. Understanding your strengths and weaknesses when it comes to looking at the future will help you understand where, and how, to start becoming more future-ready. By changing the way you think about the future, and the way you *think about* thinking about the future, you can enhance your planning strategies and skills. It may not seem so at first, but we've found that anxiety actually seems to decrease when people face what lies ahead.

So how do you know if you have a high FQ? Don't panic. Start with the easy quiz below to see how future-ready you really are.

Future Quotient quiz

1. How open would you say you are to 'looking outside' and paying attention to the broader political, economic and social trends that could affect your future?
   a. I'm very in-tune.
   b. I pay attention when I can.
   c. I'm a navel-gazer.

2. Do you have a system, or at least a mental order, for making notes for how high-level changes (in the economy, in technology, etc.) might affect you?
   a. Yes, I react consistently.
   b. I might make an adjustment or two.
   c. No. I have enough on my plate.

3. Where do you get your information? Are you good at filtering what you hear and learn about?
   a. I follow what's going on in the news, academia and the blogosphere.
   b. I tend to read those publications that relate to my job or hobbies.

    c. I have an excellent filter: only those things I want to hear get through.

4. How much effort do you put into setting goals for your future?

    a. I have a clear plan.

    b. I have a vague vision for my future.

    c. I think planning ruins the romance of life.

5. If someone asked you, 'where will you be in 5 years', how would you feel?

    a. I'd be ready to explain.

    b. I'd feel put on the spot and might need a few moments to come up with something.

    c. I'd smile and say, 'You tell me!'.

6. How open are you to recalibrating your future plans when something new pops up?

    a. I'm happy to re-evaluate. Because I've given some thought to different things which might happen, I usually feel prepared.

    b. I'm always open. The more options, the better.

    c. The judges wouldn't know talent if it hit them in the face.

7. How good do you feel you are at rational decision-making?

    a. My motto is *'Live long and prosper'*.

    b. If you ignore them for long enough, most decisions make themselves.

    c. It doesn't matter how long I spend, I always wish I'd got a different sandwich.

8. How easily can you find a path forward in your career?

    a. I am on a path I set and reset regularly.

b. I try to be flexible, but sometimes that ends in disappointment.

c. Do you know anyone who's hiring?

9. My friends and family would say that I approach the future...

a. ...with practicality and enthusiastic vision.

b. ...with my eyes closed: I rely on instinct.

c. ...only when there's nowhere left to hide.

10. When an unexpected event changes my situation, I react by:

a. Adjusting my plan accordingly – this is why I plan!

b. Getting grumpy, but assuming that things will work themselves out.

c. Total meltdown. Why does this always happen to me?

With any luck you've come through this quiz unscathed. How did you do?

Mostly **a**s – Congratulations on choosing this book to further refine your high FQ.

Mostly **b**s – Don't worry, help is at hand.

Mostly **c**s – Oh my goodness. Still, some hope, I guess. You were smart enough to open this book. Baby steps...

A light-hearted quiz, but with some serious thinking behind it. What did you learn about yourself? Is your future something you consider carefully? Do you think there is room for improvement? Consider this: if a work colleague or your boss asked you these kinds of questions about your department's targets for the year, you'd have no trouble in coming up with an answer. Yet when it comes to the future of your own life, that engagement and responsiveness just seems to fade away.

Unless you are the fiendish villain in a film, it is always better to have a clear view of the future, of different possible futures. (If you are the villain, then you will have spoken your cunning plan out loud, revealing your psychotic ambition and also how the plan will inevitably be foiled.) This book's objective is to try to help normal and very smart people like you increase your Future Quotient. Futureal's approach with clients is to use logic and creativity to think both broadly about what factors will impact the future, and specifically about how these factors may affect their company's future. It makes sense for individuals as well. By the end of this book, we hope the fear will have been somewhat taken out of your future. Better to come prepared, however the party turns out.

2

Future Philosophy

Can we ever know the future?

No! But as this book will hopefully persuade you, just because you can't predict the future with certainty is not a reason to ignore it. In fact, this very uncertainty is all the more reason to take the time to think about your future. It could turn out in so many strikingly different ways. You owe it to your future self to do some future planning, to take the time every now and then to stop and consider where you are taking yourself.

Projections vs predicting

'If a black cat crosses your path,
it signifies that the animal is going somewhere.'
Groucho Marx

Have you ever been to a fortune-teller? A bit embarrassing, but once, yes? Maybe you were curious and made a tipsy, investigative phone call to a classified ad, or were dragged along by a needy friend, or you accepted the offer from someone in an outlandish outfit to read your palm at a party? (If you have your fortune-teller on speed dial, this is not the book for you.) The astrology pages remain one of the most popular sections in newspapers and magazines, couched in language sufficiently vague to somehow apply to most of the readers, who anyway only tend to remember the predictions which turned out to be right. (As you can see, I am sceptical about astrology, but a friend tells me apparently that is because I am a Gemini – no way out).

What seems to most impress people about fortune-tellers and tarot card readers is the sense that they have been profoundly understood. That someone has seen through the social veneer to the 'real person' beneath, illuminating their fears and hopes. I think the logic is that once someone has proven (or given the sense, at least) that they have a particular vision into the secrets of you, then they also have the ability to see into the secrets of your future – which they will share with you, usually for a small fee. In this, the subject may well have fallen for what is known as the Forer or Barnum Effect, where people have a tendency to accept vague and general personality descriptions as highly accurate if they believe these descriptions have been tailored to them.

The future, and knowing the future, exerts an incredibly compelling draw for people. In films and books where someone is given a special insight into the future, they usually try to turn it to their advantage, tilting the laws of probability unfairly in their favour – choosing the winning lottery numbers, buying or dumping company shares. But there is an interesting moral twist to most of these tales. The character who knows too much usually ends up wrong-footed, caught in a trap of destiny, or simply unable to bear the burden of their extra knowledge, especially if it is certainty as to the time and manner of their death. They try to cheat destiny, but in a pre-determined world when all they have done is read the writing on the wall, the future is fixed. Greek myth and Grimm stories are full of examples of fools who try to defy the certainty of an oracle. The wicked queen in Snow White was always going to get it in the end.

What lies at the centre of all of this is a belief that the future is fixed, and prescience (seeing ahead) is possible. All that is required to gain foresight is a smart, gifted, divine or sensitive-enough eye. Come what may, events will unfold as they are meant to. Ultimately, fate cannot be cheated. Many people are open to this way of thinking and at least once a year someone, somewhere, has decoded a mysterious set of signs to arrive at a very certain end date for the world. This provides a wonderful source of entertainment for sceptics as we watch those who believe themselves to be 'in the know' prepare and rant against all of us fools who don't see it coming. Again. How far will they go? Will they hedge their bets *at all*? But then as the day of the apocalypse rolls by uneventfully, we get to watch their videos on YouTube explaining how on earth they read the signs slightly wrong, and actually it's all going to kick off next year. The end of the world, it turns out, is *always* nigh.

Science fiction may offer a more flexible and fluid version of the future, open to change and curious plot twists by time travellers. Think of H.G. Wells' Time Traveller in *The Time Machine*, Marty McFly trying to get his parents to meet when he goes *Back to the Future*, John Connor rescuing his younger self in *Terminator*, or the adventures of *Doctor Who*. But despite our desire for certainty, we can only take so much.

There is a raft of websites (www.deathclock.com, www.deathdate. info etc) which, once you've put in a few relevant points about your health and outlook, promise to predict the exact date of your death. Once you know about it, it's hard to resist the urge to give it a try. I believe these sites attract us out of morbid curiosity, but we like that we know they are just guessing. If we really thought that the site was right, and could accurately predict our death date, how many people would really want to know? How many could cope with that information? It seems less tempting now, surely. Even Texan company Life Length, which for $700 will scan your

DNA to tell you how long you will live, has a disclaimer against being able to predict you being run over by a bus.

One of the things which makes it so difficult to think about the future is the uncertainty, the possibilities, the 'what ifs...'. Uncertainty is uncomfortable, fragile, like treading on shaky ground. But when it comes to mortality, the only way we can function is with a little bit of that uncertainty. It turns out that certainty, too, is something we can't always deal with. To some extent, when someone knows the exact time of their death, they are robbed of life. The certain and fixed is less attractive than the infinitely possible. Could this be why people might stall at handing over $700 to Life Length?

Where do you want to go tomorrow?

The other wonderful thing about the future is no one can tell you you're wrong about it – at least not now. Utopian dreams have a long and distinguished history, projected on to a more enlightened or fairer or stricter or goodness-knows-how-but-somehow better future when the problems of today have been radically sorted. Plato came up with perhaps the earliest utopian proposal in his *Republic*. Containing discussion as to the best way to ensure justice and good governance, there are some elements which some may have found less appealing, such as the state-controlled human breeding programme. Mates, for example, would be chosen by a marriage number, a quantitative assessment of their quality so that high quality people would interbreed to create very high quality. Not everyone's cup of tea.

The most famous utopia of all is Thomas More's, which gave the name to the genre. The original Latin name for his book has been translated as *A Truly Golden Little Book, No Less Beneficial Than Entertaining, of the Best State of a Republic, and of the New Island*

Utopia, which points to the book being designed as as much a story as a political manifesto. Edward Bellamy, who wrote the hugely successful *Looking Backward, 2000-1887*, published in 1888, said he had wanted to write 'a literary fantasy, a fairy tale of social felicity'[6], but that didn't prevent thousands of people taking it as a manifesto for change and setting up Nationalist Clubs all over the US inspired by Bellamy's socialist vision of nationalised industry.

However, the thing which unites all utopias is that real people, with all their ugly habits and lowly drives, can't live in them. As John Carey puts it in the *Faber Book of Utopias*, 'In a utopia, real people cannot exist, for the very obvious reason that real people are what constitute the world that we know, and it is that world which every utopia is designed to replace'[7]. People living in utopias are amazingly unselfish and there is little criminality. The criminals have vanished, or the criminal impulse has been quashed, or they have been put to good use (household slaves in More's *Utopia*). Or they have become better humans, to the point (for example) in Edward Bellamy's *Looking Backward* where the criminals would refuse to lie to avoid being punished.

Authors resort to all sorts of different devices to improve their future characters. H.G. Wells' '*In the Days of the Comet*' has a comet coming close to earth and somehow magnetising out all the bad bits of humanity. In Aldous Huxley's *Island*, the anti-social just need to take two pink pills after meals and they are back to (ab)normal. Some people might see this as a fairly accurate prediction of life today.

As with all visions of the future, utopias tell us much about the author and the time when they were writing; from Plato's eugenics,

---

6   Bellamy, Edward. 'Why I Wrote Looking Backward', The Nationalist, vol. 2, 1890.
7   Carey, John. Faber Book of Utopias. London: Faber and Faber, 2000.

to Thomas More's advocating the abolition of difference in dress and housing against the backdrop of a society obsessed with the display of wealth and finery, to Edward Bellamy's pointed prediction that the future utopia of 2000 would be free of lawyers, whom he hated.

The future, of course, can also provide the perfect backdrop to dystopia, utopia's hellish twin. Here authors can explore their fears and sound a warning to society about the direction in which they think it might be going. George Orwell's *1984* is the dystopia which seems to have the most powerful stranglehold on the popular imagination, with its visions of a totalitarian society constantly under surveillance seeming to prefigure CCTV, reality television and the ubiquity of camera phones. His vision is unrelentingly grim, ' "If you want a picture of the future of humanity imagine a boot stamping on a human face — for ever." Memory would be abolished, history rewritten and language controlled.'[8]

In Aldous Huxley's *Brave New World*, 'civilisation is sterilisation'. The Director of the Central London Hatchery proudly explains how the principle of mass production has been applied to biology, making natural procreation obsolete. Embryos are sent to the Social Predestination Room to be conditioned into one of five possible social classes, from the super-intelligent Alpha down to Epsilons, who 'do the dirty work and obey', an echo rising up from the past for current fears about designer babies and unbridgeable social inequality. At least in Huxley's world some diversion and fun can be had with a trip to the 'feelies' (multi-sensory cinema) or some hallucinogenic *soma*.

It's extreme but somehow believable and that's the amazing thing about the future. It can, in this sense, be whatever you want

8   Crick, Bernard. *George Orwell: A Life*. London: Secker & Warburg, 1982.

it to be (or not be), as long as you can take people with you through the power of your logic or the story.

It ain't necessarily so

These utopian and dystopian visions tend to be self-consciously described as stories rather than predictions, but as we have seen regarding people who believe in crystal balls, tarot cards, tea leaf readings etc, for some people the future has already been decided. There is only one way things can turn out. Since the future is predetermined, it can be predicted, if only you had the right equipment. I do not believe this is right. Free will vs determinism is a mighty complicated issue, and if you really want to fight about it on a philosophical basis, we will have to take it outside. It makes overwhelming sense to me that we are all facing a multiplicity of possible futures that something causes another thing to happen. Our life paths are not set. Decisions we make today will impact our lives tomorrow and beyond. Changes in the world around us will change our circumstances.

This is not to say that we must inhabit the opposite extreme and constantly confront ourselves with the idea of a future of such infinite uncertainty and variety that nothing can be counted on. That model of the future is one of complete chaos. Just contemplating the infinite number of different forces potentially impacting on each other in an infinite number of ways can lead to paralysis and a sense of exhaustion. This model is neither workable nor constructive. There are some things we have to assume or we cannot live our daily lives: continuity of sustenance, shelter, people who are close to us, the ground beneath our feet. None of these things are certain: we may well face earthquakes or lose our homes and loved ones. However, continuously exploring our fears would make it impossible to move forward. Rather, there is a way we can sensibly 'order' the future into those things which we should consider and question and those which we must take as read.

Glorious uncertainty

One of the aims of this book, then, is to get the reader to become more comfortable with uncertainty. To embrace it, even. Instead of desperately and blindly focusing on the certainties of the future, the hope is that an acceptance of the uncertainties of how your life is going to turn out will allow you to investigate them with some degree of objectivity. Through this process you can confront and prepare for the uncertainties of life, arriving at a smarter and more useful way to plan and prepare for your future. This approach cannot promise to eliminate stress, but perhaps it can turn more of it to *eustress*[9], positive stress, a feeling of fulfilment which can come from exploring potential gains and the effort required to do so, and which encourages you to move forward.

In turbulent times, people seem to worship certainty, or at least the appearance of it, like stuffing money into a mattress. However, like other 'sticking plaster' solutions which provide superficial comfort, stuffing money in the mattress may not be quite the certain bet that it seems, given it is not immune to inflation, the typical outcome of financial flux. Certainty in these cases is irrational, but uncertainty is associated with weakness, certainty with conviction and confidence. Political manifestos must be full of intent not hypotheticals. Politicians and business leaders have to stride into the future confidently, no wavering allowed. This sense of certainty, of a strong belief at least, goes for all gurus too if they want to attract a following (although depending on their mystical

---

9   A term first used by the endocrinologist Hans Selye in 1975, to contrast with *distress*.

quotient, they are permitted to couch their pronouncements with ambiguity, requiring interpretation).

This preference for certainty may be understandable. Some fearful patients may not be able to deal with, or in any way be helped by, knowing the depth of their physician's uncertainty. A judge pronouncing sentence on a criminal who, five minutes earlier, before the verdict had been delivered, was just a person accused, must emphatically state that (s)he did it, no more doubts now, reasonable or otherwise.

How do we select in whom to place our trust? 'The public' demands assurance. Training for public speaking and addressing the media tells you how you can respond to a question to which you don't know the answer in such a way as to bring you back to safer, confident ground. Do anything but admit you don't know. But when it comes to the future, it is the only honest way to be.

Behind closed boardroom doors, away from the shareholders' AGM and the financial results briefing, corporate uncertainty is allowed to some degree. It is essential if the company is to survive the vagaries of the future. Every IPO[10] prospectus has a 'Risks' section, where the company shows it has formally considered the risks it might be facing, and how it might address them.

When it comes to us as individuals, admitting – embracing, even – some uncertainty and working with it and through it to allow the possibility of multiple futures to present themselves is a mighty powerful and effective way to prepare for whatever is to come. The Futureal strapline, if it can be said to have one, is 'it's not about being right, it's about being ready'. It's useful because it helps us get across that we don't pretend to be able to predict the future, and that it is more important to have thought through the

---

10   Initial Public Offering, the first time a company sells stock to the public.

different things which might happen and be ready for them than attempt precise predictions where you are bound to fail. What is possible? What is probable? What is preferable? For this reason, many large corporations have whole departments devoted to risk analysis, running models and simulations to envisage and plan for likely and less likely scenarios.

And there is no doubt that not everyone enjoys the process, at least initially. As Mike Roberts, co-founder of LYFE Kitchen, a new healthy restaurant concept, and former President of McDonalds described the process of future planning: 'Even in that comfortable room that you find yourself in, you can feel in that room the tension of people going outside of their comfort zone saying "what if our product is being replaced as we sit here in a garage somewhere in San Francisco?" In a year, our product no longer matches up with our customer. It's an uncomfortable place to be sitting, but it's only in that environment that the planning process becomes robust. In that space, in the tension between future and present is where innovation takes place.'[11]

Why think about the future?

Why not? Really, how could you not? So many people end up spending hours every year selecting their lunchtime sandwich, researching which app to download, worrying about getting the tiles just right. Starbucks proudly claims it offers 87,000 drink permutations, someone somewhere is poring over the almost 4,000 options they have been offered by Amazon.com when they searched for 'doilies'. We invest our time and attention into these small and often transient things, and then skim over, or blunder through, the really big decisions which are going to change our lives.

---

11 In conversation with the author.

And if *you* are not going to think about your future, who is? Because if there is one thing that is certain about the future, it is that it is coming. (Unless you are sure about the Rapture and the End of Time, in which case, again, this is probably not the book for you. Don't forget to turn out the lights when you leave.)

We all know people who seem to be continuously surprised by the way things turn out. The understanding of their own lives is strewn with quirky twists of fate, unexpected responses, curveballs and unintended consequences. 'Well, I didn't see that coming...' Well, did they even try?

You owe it to yourself to take a bit of time to think through the possible outcomes of your actions and your decisions. You won't see all of the outcomes transpire – you may not even see *most* of them happen, in fact –, but this is about an attitude, taking a mental stance against a kind of vagueness and confusion in your personal life that would be unacceptable in your professional one.

At best, using this process can lay out for you a number of different scenarios for how your life can unfold, so you can be better prepared. At worst, knowing that you properly considered your actions and potential outcomes means you can limit the pain of regret. The aim is to get all of us to become futurists about our own lives, as described by Wendell Bell, futurist and Professor Emeritus at Yale University: 'Futurists, the practitioners of the futures field, aim to demystify the future, to make their methods explicit, to be systematic and rational, to base their results on the empirical observation of reality where relevant, and to test rigorously the plausibility of their logic in open discussion and intellectual debate.'[12]

12　Bell, Wendell. *Foundations of Future Studies, Volume 1.* Piscataway, New Jersey: Transaction Publishers, 1996.

It's no secret

Can individuals change their own future? The pre-determined view says no. On the other hand, the extreme of personal empowerment thinking has us as total Masters of Our Universes. Everything is within our grasp, if only we wish for it enough. This can be dangerous thinking. In his book *SHAM*, Steve Salerno says the self-help and actualisation movement does irreparable damage by preaching the philosophy of empowerment which exalts attitude over achievement[13]. Beyond this, does it mean that if things do not work out the way we want it is entirely our fault? It must surely lead to disappointment.

This is not to disrespect the potential benefits of positive thinking. Planning and a positive outlook can sense opportunity. However, at an extreme (and especially for vulnerable people), overly positive thinking can cross into delusion. This book won't be able to tell you whether you can dance or not, but it does stress the importance of trying to get some degree of objectivity about you and your potential before you sell the family silver to pay for the ticket to an *X Factor* audition.

One of the key skills essential to thinking about your own future is the ability to identify those things which are within your control, and those which are beyond it. There are other books to help you deal emotionally with things being within and out of your control. This book is designed to provide you with a practical way to plan through both what you can and cannot control, and makes a starting assumption that you realise you don't control the world, fabulous and powerful as you may well be (and an excellent dancer).

---

13 Salerno, Steve. *SHAM: How the Self-Help Movement Made America Helpless*. New York: Crown, 2005.

Help Yourself

'I went to a bookstore and asked the saleswoman,
"Where's the self-help section?" She said if she told me,
it would defeat the purpose.'
– George Carlin

Where did you buy this book? I'm not asking whether it was in Rome Airport or Waterloo station. I mean, what section of the on- or offline bookstore? I was very relieved it was going to be sold in the business section, as self-help has become something of an off-putting label for many people. If you found it in 'Mind, Body Spirit', then it may have been miscatalogued, and I'm sure you were just passing through. I'm afraid that you will find little to nourish the body or spirit here. 'Personal effectiveness', however, is fine, although would a rose by any other name smell as sweet (or be as useful?). How has the meaning of self-help moved so far from just helping yourself?

The term self-help first appeared in 1859, coined in the UK by the Scottish writer and philosopher Samuel Smiles. It expressed the contemporary idea that people could take charge of their own lives and shape their futures[14]. Smiles was writing at a time when the social effects of the industrial revolution were creating new social classes, mobility and rules. In some ways, the development of the self-help genre mirrors a breakdown and fragmentation in existing traditions and social norms. With social change came the prospect of new possibilities and uncertainty, and the need for new sources of authority on how to behave and navigate life.

---

14 Smiles, Samuel. *Self Help.* (Oxford World Classics series.) Oxford: Oxford University Press, 2008.

In 1859, Frederick Engels had recently revealed the terrible *Conditions of the Working Class in England* and Dickens was writing about *Hard Times*. There was much room for improvement. *Self Help* follows a narrative formula still highly familiar to any viewers of Oprah and readers of self-help articles in not-very-glossy magazines: tales of an unpromising start and discouragement are followed by triumph in the face of adversity leading to wealth and social acclaim. Where Smiles' version diverts from current self-help narrative is in the fact that success after death counts for something, whereas contemporary self-help and business tales of triumph require some evidence of success in this life, ideally as glossy as possible.

Another self-help classic, Dale Carnegie's book *How to Win Friends and Influence People*, is still in the Amazon Top 100 more than 70 years after it was published in 1937. The genre really took off in the 1960s, with the last few decades seeing an explosion in the number of self-help books published. In the 1970s, having and using a middle initial became an important requirement for being taken seriously as a self-help or personal effectiveness author, especially in the US[15]. You can't go into a bookshop without being confronted with row upon row of titles featuring phrases such as 'self-empowerment', 'the real you' and 'inner power'. The popularity of such books has grown as individuals are confronted with what the sociologist Emile Durkheim referred to as *anomie*, an absence of social norms. Feeling a lack of empathy or sound advice from those around them, people turn elsewhere, looking for *The Rules* or even just to be told 'He's just not that into you'[16].

---

15 This book was written by Tamar A. Kasriel.
16 Interestingly, on Amazon.co.uk, the following from the *Daily Express* is showcased in the review section of *He's Just Not That Into You* as something to shout about: 'Sometimes an idea for a new book is so blindingly obvious that we think we should have written it ourselves.'

There are many books to tell individuals how to improve their lives, set goals, become more personally effective/assertive/alluring or even improve their self-help book writing skills[17]. However, for some, the whole self-help genre is tarnished with mysticism, irrationality, get-rich-quick schemes and broken promises. If one of them worked for all, if we were all in a state of universal bliss, the genre would no longer exist, killed by its own success. Maybe the self-help writers' union have worked this out so they deliberately withhold the real secret of success which is to write self-help books which only tell you a part of the secret.

So what's new?

Three things are new now: access to new types of information in new ways, a particular pitch and intensity of uncertainty in the world around us, and an openness and interest in some aspects of business and the corporate world which makes individuals newly competent to appreciate and use corporate techniques. People now have particular access to information, to crowdsourcing, which is changing the background to decision-making, and the potential to access new relevant information and expertise. In a globalised and flatter world, the range of factors that can impact on *your* future is far greater. All of these point to an appetite and a need for better individual future planning.

There's a shared sense across many different sectors and interest groups that a failure to plan ahead is going to have severe consequences. This concern over the fine mess we have gotten ourselves into and the urgent need for a really good plan to find our way out goes well beyond individual companies, and has made

---

17   Stine, Jean Marie. *Writing Successful Self-help and How-to Books*. Hoboken, New Jersey: Wiley, 1997.

all sorts of people open to confronting *the Inconvenient Truth*. As Dr Philipp Rode, who heads up the Cities programme at London School of Economics, put it: 'We are currently going through a very interesting period in the broader political context where I would suggest there is a revival of planning...we are becoming aware that daily muddling through will fail to deliver some of the more transformative changes that are required...In this particular moment, we should be taking advantage of mankind's capacity for working very strategically, thinking ahead, doing planning properly. Otherwise, we will find ourselves in a situation where the future will shock us...in a situation in which one wakes up in the morning and finds oneself completely unprepared[18].' It is no coincidence that many of the most enthusiastic and thoughtful champions of long-term planning today are to be found within the environmental movement. The fear that as a species we are hurtling to hell in a handbasket provides a remarkably powerful inducement to plan.

In a spin/I'm so dizzy

'We are living in an era of unprecedented change.' How often have you heard this? Do you feel it? In some ways it is always true, at least the 'unprecedented' part. But every era, every generation seems to have felt that change is faster than ever before, and that we are being faced with hitherto unimaginable pressures to keep up, compared to the relative calm and comfort of previous generations.

The question is not whether things are changing or not (they are), but whether there has been a qualitative shift in the *pace* of change. Is change really accelerating, or do we just perceive it that way? Ray Kurzweil, one of the most prominent and provocative

---

thinkers about the future, talks about the concept of the 'singularity', 'a future period during which the pace of technological change will be so fast and far-reaching that human existence on this planet will be irreversibly altered'.[19] He stresses that most people don't see these changes or believe that they are coming because they are under the false impression that change is linear rather than exponential.

Bicycle face

When the bicycle was first invented, there was a genuine fear that the human body was not designed to go at such speeds and that, if you went on a bicycle, you were putting yourself at risk of permanent physical disfigurement. What is happening now is a particular and powerful combination of factors which are multiplying the affects of change to push us to what may feel like the limits of human adaptability. This can be a scary prospect, and, especially as people age, they can become fearful of the future. But is it just a new version of bicycle face? These same dynamics (minus the microchips) were at work in the Industrial Revolution in eighteenth and nineteenth century Europe – technological change coming in the form of a spinning jenny, say, rather than call centres or supermarket self-checkout or Twitter, but with huge social, economic and political implications, and leaving many scared for their future and livelihoods.

Moore's Law, the much quoted theory from Intel co-founder Gordon Moore, holds that the technological capacity of microchips will double every 18 months. Frequently scrutinised, sometimes debunked, often confirmed, this theory is quoted so often because

---

19 Kurzweil, Ray. 'Reinventing humanity: The future of human–machine intelligence,' *The Futurist*, March-April 2006.

it sums up the sense of ever increasing speed of technological change. Change in this one sphere then has a rapid, knock-on effect in other spheres (social, economic, political). For some, that means a future where the machines run the show. According to Justin Rattner of Intel, 'we may be approaching an inflection point where the rate of technology advancements is accelerating at an exponential rate, and machines could even overtake humans in their ability to reason, in the not so distant future'.[20]

Whether we are facing an *I, Robot* future or something more benign, the critical element in all of this is the fact that change is now *exponential*. The concept of exponential growth may be explained using the fable of the courtier who asked the king that in exchange for his gift of a chessboard, the king give him one grain of rice for the first square on the chessboard, two for the second, four for the third and so on, doubling the amount of rice each time. By the time the twenty-first square is reached, a million grains are required, and all the rice in the world is insufficient by the time one reaches the last squares. We cannot reduce this sense of exponential change to which we are subject to a neat formula, but perhaps it is best described as the sense of a steep gradient which is getting steeper all the time.

Interesting things can happen when gradients change. Within demography, some thinkers have posited the model of 'actuarial escape velocity', when recent gains on extending life expectancy reach such a pace that they increase by more than one year every year. According to the folks at the Methuselah Foundation (the clue's in the name), this could see some people living to hundreds of years, if not indefinitely.

---

20 'Intel CTO Predicts Singularity by 2050', http://www.engadget.com/2008/08/22/intel-cto-predicts-singularity-by-2050/

But what does this all mean for the above average person who has bought this book, making decisions about the future? At the very least, we should be prepared that those systems and technologies underpinning our professional and personal lives might change. Technology will get 'better' but this progress might mean that tools we have invested in might become obsolete or that we will require new training to keep up with the times.

Human drivers and the place of nostalgia

'We have normality. I repeat, we have normality. Anything you still can't cope with is therefore your own problem.'
– **Douglas Adams**

Today, the constant message is that the world is in a phase of unprecedented disruption, that successful individuals will be those who can embrace uncertainty and collect skills which they can turn, chameleon-like, to whatever demands and opportunities arise. Certainty and the job for life is dead, long live ambiguity. But the importance of adaptability is not a new idea. Darwin is credited as the first one to say 'it is not the strongest of the species that survives; nor the most intelligent that survives. It is the one that is most adaptable to change'. This idea has not been invented by people with really cool shoes.

Yet the current wave of Titans, masters of technology, marching confidently into goodness knows what, headsets soon to be replaced by gestures and shouting at gadgets whose voice recognition still needs a bit of work, have moments of doubt. Change can be exciting and broadens the horizons of opportunity beyond what is imaginable, but even the person who is enjoying the ride has moments of terror. For the majority, we would like to step slowly into the water, test it out, see how it feels and battle a truly human sense of nostalgia for the way things *felt* – if not for how they *were*.

It would be foolish to deny the power of nostalgia in colouring our mindset and how we feel about an uncertain future. If you are one of the many who find the future daunting, however well you may hide it, rather than suggesting that you perform major surgery on yourself and rip out your need for a sense of continuity, I suggest that you acknowledge it. Yes, many things are changing and paradigms are flashing by before we've even had a chance to open them, but a key part of the processes outlined in this book involve highlighting continuity as much as disruption. Furthermore, when it comes to our personal strategies, change or intervention are not, ipso facto, automatically the better options. But if you are maintaining the status quo in the face of uncertainty, it should be because you've worked out it doesn't need fixing, not because you can't bear to think about anything else.

And continuity is there if we look for it however much the mantra of change and disruption is preached by the wizards of silicon valley and the zippy commentators, even if we have to go back to a base level of human needs like communication and bonding to find it (see Chapter 4). As a consultancy involved in helping companies anticipate and deal with change, Futureal works from the assumption that technology has to initially fulfil an existing human need to be widely taken up. Once it is embedded in our social fabric, only then does it start to change how we operate as humans. To take an obvious example, mobile phones took off initially because they fulfilled a basic human need – to communicate. It is only with their ubiquity that they have changed *how* we communicate.

Continuity does not make news. Change is exciting and cutting edge. But for those people whose knuckles are truly white from gripping the sides of the roller coaster (if you have even dared to get on), the techniques outlined later in this book are about imagining a sensible, logical, iterative path through uncertainty. By accepting the variability of the future and thoughtfully examining from a position of knowledge about yourself and your environment, a guide rope can be constructed through uncertain terrain.

In businesses facing disruption and uncertainty, if one goes in with a bulldozer and is too brutal with the change message some people will just stop listening. It is a delicate and important thing – the person who brought you in as a consultant to help the organisation face the future may not be representative. Whilst he or she may applaud your Scary Future message, ultimately you won't be effective for the organisation if you can't take the whole team, including the more fearful, with you.

Printed cupcakes

It is a challenge for futurists. We can't go into an organisation, speak on a platform with a message that 'yes, tomorrow is going to look quite like today in some ways'. We are brought in for 'shock and awe'. And to be fair, there are a lot of bloody amazing things on the horizon. But it always comes back to people, and has to come back to people if we are to get the audience to imagine themselves living in this brave new world. Otherwise, it just remains a kind of abstract science fiction from which it is difficult to build corporate strategy.

To illustrate, one of the things which really got people thinking five years ago was the advent of 3D printers. For a few months, those at the leading edge of the futurist circuit were enjoying the appreciative buzz of early-adopter audiences as they computed for themselves what the ability to replicate anything on a micro, personal scale could really mean. Now this niche audience has heard it all before, but some of the first 3D printers are coming out and into the public space, and at CES (Consumer Electronics Show) this year the big noise was about printing...chocolate cupcakes. The best way, it turns out, to fire up people's interest in this fantastic technology turns out to be a mundane, human-scale snack.

Work it out

At work we all learn to behave slightly differently than we do when we are 'at home', even if we work from home. In a work environment, we are sensible and accountable. We try to look at things objectively. When challenged, we can justify decisions rationally. Some aspects of how we are at work could be useful for who we are at home, but there is a sense that outlook and behaviour should be different at home and at work. At home, we *should* be free of work constraints and hierarchies, we *should* express our true feelings and act on them. So when it comes to our personal lives, somehow, perhaps because it is seen as emotional territory, so many of us abandon any attempt to be objective, to step outside ourselves, to truly make sense of our decisions, even though we could potentially gain so much if we distilled the right things from our work mentality and applied them here.

Intuition and impulse are fine in the personal sphere, but they can also be detrimental. Thoughtless decisions come back to haunt us, both in their outcomes and in their very thoughtlessness. As Professor Kahneman said in our interview 'One of the things that thinking deeply can do, even if it doesn't lead to better decisions, is inoculate you against regret, and later on you can travel back to the point at which you made the decision and understand and come to terms with the decision you have made.' We live our daily lives in the wake of decisions made without sufficient consideration. We talk, chat, gossip and speculate about so many things which may be unrelated to our own lives, and then tend to neglect the future of that which is most important, which will have the biggest impact on us.

With great power comes great responsibility

There is a sound principle of psychology around the idea of the 'locus of control', which refers to the extent to which an individual feels they can control things which affect them.[21] This perception turns out to be a function of personality, with 'Internals' at one end of a continuum believing they have more control over what happens to them, and 'Externals' less. (We will explore this in a bit more detail in Chapter 5.)

Taking control over one's own life is a key axiom of the self-help doctrine of personal empowerment. This is often taken too far, in my view. I'm not convinced there is 'a secret'. Believing in and chanting your power over your environment, your magnetism for money you haven't got or people you haven't yet met is proof of your chanting ability, not proof of your power.

However, wherever you place the fault line between sensible assessment of your impact and control over your world and misguided delusion, the decisions you make today will have an impact on your life tomorrow. With the power you do have over your future comes a responsibility to take some of those decisions seriously, and not to neglect them in favour of easier and maybe more entertaining dilemmas.

---

21 The 'locus of control' theory was first introduced by psychologist Julian B. Rotter in 1954 and was further developed by Rotter, Bernard Weiner and others.

Where's the romance?

This book proposes a rational approach, a search for the holy grail of objectivity on our own lives where the quest, the process, is in some ways as important as the goal. Wouldn't that take all the romance and excitement out of life? How about spontaneity, surprise, kicking off your shoes and being fancy-free, taking whatever life throws at you? Aren't we at risk of analysing and planning all the surprises out?

I don't believe so. Knowing how a clock or car works doesn't make it less beautiful as a machine. Knowing the chemical triggers for, and responses of, love doesn't diminish the feeling. Trying to get a sense of some of the causes and effects which are shaping our worlds doesn't make the journey any less interesting and worthwhile. People who trumpet the joys of spontaneity tend to forget that not everything spontaneous is also fun – break-ups and repossession orders can also come out of the blue.

More positively, serendipity can and will strike. Future planning is about *managing* uncertainty: it cannot and should not promise to remove it.

3

How Companies Plan

There is no universal, fool-proof solution for how all businesses can succeed. This issue is exacerbated by the extent of uncertainty and turbulence which the corporate world, actually the whole world, is going through. Yet however much chaos and uncertainty there may be, one thing which companies have to do is plan. They may not do it well, they may not do it thoroughly and they are unlikely to do it often enough, but no company can survive just day-to-day. Foresight in its most general terms is a central ingredient in business success. At time of writing, Kodak is the latest high-profile casualty who failed to see what was coming until it was too late. Foresight can't compete with hindsight on accuracy, but is rather more useful.

Dream on

Profiles of great companies love to include a portrait of the founder(s) before they made it big, struggling as they shivered or sweated in their garret/garage. Rank amateurs surrounded by nothing but debts and doubting voices and nurtured by their dreams, they were able to live on drive and persistence until they got their first big break and the world woke up. But while dreams are an essential part of the myth, and there is no questioning the motivating power of a compelling vision, a dream will stay a dream unless you have a way to get there.

The UK TV programme *Dragons' Den* is a fascinating study in dream-squashing. Five successful business 'dragons' scrutinise from black leather thrones as a parade of wannabe entrepreneurs unveil their dreams of future success. One by one, the victims showcase their world-changing egg poachers or revolutionary de-icers, as the dragons wring out their business plans. If the hopefuls are very lucky, a dragon or two will offer some investment, but on the condition that the entrepreneurs give up sizeable equity (thus minimising the likelihood of screwing up the whole venture, amateurs that they are).

It is a powerful, if painful, reminder of the place of dreams in business – useful at times, but not enough on their own, and at worst they can be distracting and obstructive. And no good if you can't turn them into a vision which compels others to get on board. Businesses never seem to bring in motivational speakers from *inside* the business. There seems to be implicit recognition that dreams and fighting against impossible odds are to be done outside the business environment (climbing mountains or exploring the Earth's poles with as little assistance as possible), and need distilling into a short speech and some nice slides with strategy implications before they can be of any use.

What's the secret?

The business shelves are full of books promising to expose the secrets of successful companies, or the real stories behind the myths. Some of these titles offer careful analysis suggesting how companies get from *Good to Great* or *Great by Choice*, how they can be *Built to Last*, and continue to succeed. Other authors have found success highlighting the false reasoning behind these kinds of books, showing their creators were confused by *The Halo Effect* and *Fooled by Randomness*, misidentifying correlation as causality, misleadingly judging leadership on narrowly defined outcomes.

So there is little consensus on the exact ingredients required for the recipe of guaranteed corporate success. Furthermore, the sense of corporate responsibility for global economic and environmental woes, and the vulnerability and even transience of individual companies and entire sectors, has robbed the corporate sector of any right to designate itself as a perfect model for improvement. Markets are in such flux and so many of the mighty fallen, that fear of hubris seems to have temporarily calmed the high-praise business book genre. *Built to Last for a Bit* or *Great to Managing OK for Now, Thanks* are unlikely to shift many copies.

However, even as we are wary of highlighting individual businesses as paragons, one thing which we can learn from companies in general is their objectivity, accountability and the need to plan. Even the most transient business, if it is to be anything other than a one-off transaction, has to plan ahead. Let's take retail as an example, a sector which most people feel they understand at a basic level (have/buy something, sell it), and suggest a newspaper kiosk as a relatively simple format. The kiosk owner needs to plan for the following at a minimum: the land/kiosk rental, reliable supply of newspapers, having enough money to pay for stock, steady customer base, footfall and price sensitivities, let alone more complicated issues of merchandising, season and event adjustment, customer retention, unsold inventory, stock return, having the right change and a collection of innocuous comments about the weather always at the ready.

As we will see, there are many parallels in how planning is important and useful for both businesses and individuals. Katerina Gould, founder of Thinking Potential, who has been coaching executives thinking about their future for seven years following a 10-year corporate career in finance, marketing and strategy, put it this way: 'Without planning, all you can know is what you don't want. You can't try to think about "What do I want? What does it look like?" because you are so stuck in your current thinking.'[22]

What is a company?

It's surprisingly hard to find a sensible, useful definition of a company. Wikipedia is, of course, there with the legal definition of a corporation, and there's no lack of organisational theory definitions ('shared culture', 'shared tasks to get to collective goals', 'hierarchy typologies') but not much to really get your teeth into and explain why a bunch of people at work get together and do stuff and make decisions in a way which they never would back at home. Companies, after all, are just a group of individuals, but individuals which are held accountable for their actions and the consequences of those actions.

I plan, therefore I am

So what sets companies apart? Companies have a responsibility to their shareholders/stakeholders to think ahead. For public companies, the whole system of stock pricing is predicated on projections of future profitability. Whilst there can be no one-size-fits-all recipe for business greatness, planning is something which all businesses have to do. The premise of this book is that there are elements from that planning *process* and the way it is carried out which are useful to individuals.

It is important to emphasise that many companies do not do enough future planning. As Alan Giles, who has worked across several businesses and is now the chairman of the active clothing and accessories brand FatFace, as well as an Associate Fellow at Oxford's Saïd Business school, pointed out, there is often

---

resistance: 'Resources are always scarce, there is always pushback: "we're too busy, it's going to cost too much." A very frequent pushback is a sort of "what's the point" question – because the future's uncertain, what's the point of thinking about it? People would rarely articulate this, but sometimes you get the feeling that they're thinking "we're not going to be here, so why worry?" 'And, as he goes on to point out, the dangers of failing to plan are significant: 'Self-evident failure, poor results, internal recrimination if you get caught having not planned something well. You get into crisis management mode, knee-jerk reaction. It's always more costly to do something if you haven't thought it through and planned it carefully. You have to throw more money at things, hire outside help.'[23]

Planning in business is far from perfect but, unlike the personal sphere, the need for planning is universally accepted and understood.

Future Flux

As with individuals, future planning has become more difficult for companies who also have to deal with the sense of existing in an era of unprecedented change and many of these changes occurring at unimaginable speed. How can you weigh risks and guard your competitive edge when the fundamental rules of your business are shifting?

Turbulence and disruption have become the tired but still painfully relevant clichés of business books and management thinking. Philip Kotler, one of the grand old men of business academia, and John A. Caslione give a sense of the weightiness of this now well established tradition and their debt to it in the introduction to their recent book *Chaotics: The Business of Managing*

---

23 In conversation with the author.

and Marketing in the Age of Turbulence[24]. A roll-call of heavyweights, there they highlight Peter Drucker's *The Age of Discontinuity,* Andy Grove's *Only the Paranoid Survive,* Alan Greenspan's *The Age of Turbulence* and Clayton Christensen's *Business Innovation and Disruptive Technology.* They describe a world where economic cycles are absent, high impacts result from unpredictable and erratic upturns and downturns, and the market and consumers lose confidence. As strategic inflection points approach ever more rapidly, businesses have to be able to spot them at ever greater speed, trying to stay calm and centred whilst uncertainty rains down like the aliens in a game of space invaders.

Every sector is now littered with the corpses and disappointment of the once great players, brought down with ever increasing speed. In just five years, Nokia and RIM had their global mobile phone crowns snatched by Apple and Samsung. It can be hard to let go. The metal sign from outside Lehman Brothers London office went for £42,050[25], bought by an anonymous phone bidder, who takes perhaps nostalgic and tender care of it. Even the young revolutionaries cannot be secure – at time of writing, Zipcar, the new reinventors on the block of the car-sharing industry (car rental as once was), are already threatened by RelayRides.

Many companies and institutions are still struggling with the legacy of the industrial era when the key business focus after profit was efficiency: making or building things or educating people at scale. Suddenly the new buzzword is 'innovate...', with the '...or die' implicit, if unspoken. And it is not enough to just innovate, you have to embrace open innovation, a requirement to throw

---

24   Kotler, Philip, and John A. Caslione. *Chaotics: The Business of Managing and Marketing in the Age of Turbulence.* New York: Amacom, 2009.

25   http://www.bloomberg.com/news/2010-09-29/lehman-signs-fetch-111-700-in-london-as-collectors-vie-for-bank-souvenirs.html

open the systems and processes and share yourself with the world, co-create where you can, invite your customers in, even though the first to look through your new transparent windows is likely to be the competitor sprung from an angle you never foresaw.

Change is difficult for any company to face. It would be incorrect to imply that companies offer a model of perfect objectivity and eager planning when confronted by chaos. The initial response at least can be fearful and emotional. As Andy Grove, the lauded CEO of Intel and its rise, describes it, 'a manager in a business that's undergoing a strategic inflection point is likely to experience a variation of the well-known stages of what individuals go through when dealing with a serious loss. This is not surprising, because the early stages of a strategic inflection point are fraught with loss – loss of your company's pre-eminence in the industry, of its identity, of a sense of control of your company's destiny, of job security'[26]. He goes on to liken the final stages of going through a strategic inflection point (his favoured term for disruption) as having the emotional, dispirited make-up of a bedraggled group of riders in old westerns as they struggle through a hostile landscape with no certain goal but knowing they can't turn back.

The new uncertainty covers an ambiguity not just in what businesses do, but how they do it. This demands a new agility in business, with constant watchfulness for the requirement of course correction as the world throws out another curveball. While it must be tempting, companies cannot afford to just 'keep their heads down'. At the extreme, in a constantly shifting world every company is a start-up, needing to learn the new rules of the game. Future planning can no longer be an excuse for the annual senior golfing jaunt. The old assumptions will no longer do for

26   Grove, Andrew S. *Only the Paranoid Survive*. New York: Doubleday, 1996.

questions with longer term impacts when your business may have morphed into something new. What hiring policy now will provide you with the skills you will need in five years' time? In the most enlightened businesses scanning the outside and making sense of what it might mean for the business becomes part of the mentality/company culture.

Mike Roberts, former President of McDonalds and now the co-founder of LYFE restaurants, captures the shift as follows: '80% of my time in leadership is spent on planning and 20% of my time is spent on executing. The leadership has to be in a sort of scout's position of looking ahead, anticipating, observing the behaviour of their customers, investors, board and putting that data together in a way that presents the road map to the future. Those businesses who manage to win in this disruptive world, it's usually a function of how that leadership is spending their time preparing their people for the future.'[27]

This 'fluency' in long-term planning also allows businesses not to be over-influenced by fads, fearfully investing in the latest social media craze because otherwise they will be left out with the dinosaurs. A long-term perspective brings a feeling for long-term value, and an understanding that you need to pause to consider what investing in that whizzy new app will actually do for your brand and the rest of the business.

Amazon's Jeff Bezos sees a very specific competitive advantage in focusing on the longer term: 'If everything you do needs to work on a three-year time horizon, then you're competing against a lot of people. But if you're willing to invest on a seven-year time horizon, you're now competing against a fraction of those people, because very few companies are willing to do that. Just by

---

27   In conversation with the author.

lengthening the time horizon, you can engage in endeavors that you could never otherwise pursue. At Amazon we like things to work in five to seven years.'[28] Bezos has on occasion had to face down shareholder criticism for putting long-term goals ahead of short-term profit, but the impressive results to date suggest he may be onto something. The Amazon empire now spans from books to retail to computing cloud and most recently the most successful touchscreen tablet after iPad.

Author Venkatesh Rao ascribes Amazon's success to a 'great game-mind...a preternatural ability to figure out which game to play, against which opponent. And once you've decided what game you're in, aligning the entire company so that it has the capacity to play that specific game better than anybody else...To have a game-mind is to be detached from the specifics of your business as it exists today...[to]not get attached to the great things you've built or achieved, and clinically ask yourself, what's the next game?'[29].

For an organisation being future-ready can also be about empowering people in the organisation to have ideas, and to feed intelligence in, in a way somewhat similar to the 1980s Japanese philosophy of *kaizen*, or gradual, continuous improvement, but with a focus on what is happening in the outside world. It can allow people at a more junior level in the company to engage with the *raison d'être* of the business and how it might change. It may be scary for bosses, but this outlook also resonates with a new world of crowdsourcing, where being able to have and articulate a point of view, and possibly having an impact on lots of people, is not the purvey only of those at the top.

28　'Jeff Bezos owns the Web in More Ways Than You Think', *Wired*, December 2011.
29　'Why Amazon is the Best Strategic Player in Tech', *Forbes*, December 2011.

Help, we need somebody

Companies tend to bring outside consultants in to help them with the future for one of two reasons:

1. Things are going incredibly well, and there is a sense of opportunity as well as some resource to invest in it – whatever it may be.

2. Prospects are looking very grim and/or blurry and the future is the only thing which might get them out of the last chance saloon.

In some cases, the future plan has been decided, and for whatever political reason an outsider is required to lend weight to the foregone conclusion, and possibly even take any flak for the decision.

In terms of specific techniques, this book focuses on scenario planning, and futurescaping as a version of it, modified so it can be used by individuals. This is a very particular type of planning.

I have found that when it comes to businesses, an interest in scenario planning reflects a culture of openness. Scenario planning is built on uncertainty. By definition the outcomes are unknown beforehand, so it is unimaginable that it would be commissioned simply to rubber-stamp a prefabricated strategy, or that a consultant could deliver something 'they made earlier' because it is done for – and usually *with* – a particular client at a particular time.

In exploring and recommending scenario planning, this book is not saying 'here is a list of things which successful companies do or are. Please go try them at home'. Rather, scenario planning is a process of managing variability, of investigating and dealing with the different variables that impact our potential futures. It is not a fool-proof solution to business or personal issues.

External benefits

Some years ago, I worked on a project for the Performance and Innovation Unit within the UK Government Cabinet Office identifying best practice in strategic futures work. We investigated a vast breadth of organisations, both public and private, to benchmark those who were being most effective in their strategic futures planning, and pinpointing why that was[30]. One of the key elements which emerged as essential to the success of futures planning was that the group doing the planning should be at a certain distance from the main organisation: close enough to be aware of, and connect to, the challenges and culture of the organisation, but sufficiently independent to look beyond its current concerns.

So the kind of clients that have engaged Futureal, for example, are experts in their sector and their own business. They are willing to question, have a sense that there are signals to decode to get a sense of future direction, and they are looking for a logical and robust way to interpret these changes for the business and work out a sensible strategy. (Futureal's clients are also incredibly smart, discerning and attractive people, with verve and panache.) They do not bring Futureal in to learn about the current state of their industry, although they do expect us to have some expertise in how change occurs, and how factors are likely to combine to explore where the industry might go in the future. We bring the outside in, highlighting the external factors and changes which are beyond their normal business concerns and which they do not have time to keep track of.

---

30 'Understanding Best Practice in Strategic Futures Work', available at www.cgee.org.br/ atividades/redirKori/748

Let yourself go

On top of that, outsiders are neutral. Beyond an obvious desire for our clients to be successful (self-serving? Yup.), we have no stake in one outcome over another, no territory to protect or career to advance. One of the benefits of looking into the longer-term future for businesses is that it can allow people involved to release themselves from the personal. According to an article in the *Wall Street Journal* in September 2011[31], the average tenure of a Fortune 500 CEO is just 4.6 years. Ask people to plan for next year or a couple of years hence, and understandably they project themselves and their corporate life in that future, with budgets to defend, colleagues to compete with and (corner) offices to decorate.

Push out a little further, to five or ten years, and suddenly the prospect that the people in the room will be different, that the majority may well have jumped company is no longer an uncomfortable, unsayable truth, but an inoffensive fact of *realpolitik*. Distance in time can allow personal concerns to fade, and for a kind of statesmanship to emerge. I've also found that deliberately removing themselves from their daily corporate concerns also allows people pause to reflect on what the company does, and its place in the wider world, and reconnect with why they wanted to work there in the first place. Uplifting stuff!

It is this objectivity, allowing rationality precedence over potentially confusing and damaging emotional drivers and fog, which is so useful for individuals to emulate.

---

31   http://blogs.wsj.com/deals/2011/09/15/why-your-ceo-could-be-in-trouble/

Far Out, Man

---

*'In today's marketplace, planning beyond who you are having
lunch with next Thursday, is very, very difficult.'*
– Rodney Fitch, Professor of Retail Design
and founder of the Fitch design agency

Long-term future planning is not the normal 'business' of
business in the same way that making widgets, cleaning carpets or
selling drinks is. It is not day-to-day in any sense of the word. I
would say that the majority of companies don't do enough of it if
they do it at all, but it cannot be the main focus for either
businesses or people. In general, sectors and functions have a
particular focus in terms of how far they look into the future.
How far they look ahead is determined by the scale and longevity
of investments companies need to make and, therefore, the
foresight their decisions require. For example, there is a reason
why Shell, the company famous for pioneering scenario planning,
was used to having to look decades into the future: oil companies
are building facilities now which must bear up against physical
and geopolitical change for the next 50 years. A wrong decision
can prove to be financially disastrous.

As Dr Philipp Rode, of LSE Cities, described the thinking of
urban planners: 'You look ahead 50–100 years for infrastructure
such as buildings, tunnels, bridges etc. You are determining quite
a bit of the future with the stuff you put in place today.'[32]

Whilst there are always exceptions, there are discernible patterns
in how companies address the future within sectors. Corporate
sectors with long lead times (for example, those building

---

32   In conversation with the author.

manufacturing facilities), have to consider materials supply and demand for the life of the facility. Retailers, on the other hand, tend to have far shorter future-planning time frames outside of building stores. It is not just that fashion changes fast, but the fact that they are able to experiment and innovate endlessly, trying out a new format or category mix on the shopfloor and able to tweak or change it instantly based on customer feedback. As Rodney Fitch pointed out: 'There's a great deal of instinct in the retail sector, a great deal of opportunism, rather more than they'd admit to. A lot of instinctive activity rather than planning...There are none of the major 10 retailers in the world that are as old as I am. Planning for more than the next two-three years is optimistic and, in the retail sector, in many ways dangerous.'[33]

For those companies which do implement scenario planning, each will carry out and use the process a little differently. Nike's Shambhala initiative, a focus on sustainable business, was kicked off (as it were) with a scenario planning process task force pulled together by Phil Knight in 1993[34], creating the Nike Environmental Action Team which focused on compliance, manufacturing and monitoring. Ford uses wildcard analysis (wildcards are low probability, high impact events; see Chapter 7) as well as trends and scenario planning to evaluate opportunities, threats and strategy for the business, leading to a turnaround for the company and its 'One Ford' strategy. Apparently Ford had 50 people writing the scenario stories, and then rewrote them in different locations around the globe. Lego generated a series of different scenarios as part of its 2009 budget, with contingency plans for each. Their Serious Play project has them using Lego toys to play out different scenarios.

---

33 In conversation with the author.
34 http://dragonflyint.com/nike/Drive/101_evolution.htm

Accountability

For any company with more than one employee, and especially a public one, planning is not a private affair. This doesn't mean a live broadcast from the boardroom strategy session, but that decisions about the future direction of the business will have been aired, scrutinised and justified. It is just too dangerous to be the lone wolf CEO ignoring the views of those around him (it is usually him) and thrusting boldly without heed to man or board. The financial pack will turn on you. At the very least, a gamble needs an audience: otherwise who will know how brave and smart you were if it all goes right? And you need to have others on whom to pass the buck if it doesn't.

What can be so difficult for new leaders of public companies is the sudden realisation of how penetrating the spotlight has become. As the zone of accountability widens to include not just shareholders but customers, the environment and even the competition, entire external comms departments have sprung up, supported by external PR agencies, to manage the message. Twitter brings a whole new front of communication (and exposure and vulnerability).

Business gets personal

There's been a lot written on how the boundaries between work and leisure are blurring, how the social technologies (Facebook, Twitter) which used to be part of one's personal life now have a place and a function at work. Pictures of the family are now *de rigueur* on the office desk and desktop wallpaper. (There is an unspoken but strict set of rules in operation here: pictures of kids – your own – are preferred, followed by a picture of your partner. Pictures of parents, for some reason, aren't cool, and pet snaps seem to be acceptable only if you work in administration. You can put up a picture of yourself only if it shows you grinning and a bit rumpled either in sporting gear – ideally clutching some sort of prop like a snowboard or crampons – or dressed as a giant rabbit for charity.)

Team-building exercises and corporate days-out encourage some revelation of the personal, as do workshop warm-ups. Yet there is still most definitely a sense that we can and should have different *modus operandi* at work and outside. Work is where we are focused and accountable and rational, non-work (home/with friends) is where we can and should allow our emotions to emerge. Despite the horrors, the time of a commute (and maybe a nice glass of wine) are needed to decompress between the two states.

Eleanor Cooksey, a life coach who specialises in younger professionals, said, 'Individuals who appear to be most successful in their professional lives can operate very differently out of work. You can see it most clearly with women in particular as they also dress very differently. One of my clients, for example, who was made a partner at a consultancy firm in her early thirties (i.e. doing very well indeed) reads the FT and The Grocer going into work, always in a suit. At weekends she likes celebrity magazines, and adopts a completely different posture, and frankly seems like a completely different person, in jeans and hippy tops.'*

As Andy Gilbert, founder of Go MAD thinking, a business improvement consultancy, points out: 'Most people can't be bothered to plan. What changes that in a work context is the work processes or work culture, e.g. my boss says I have to do this by a certain time, a business plan which needs to be delivered to the board in two weeks, someone else has asked them to plan, or someone is highly motivated by a project and can't wait to get planning.'[35]

---

*   In conversation with the author.
35   In conversation with the author.

None of your business

I'm not suggesting that corporate warriors should take their armour and battle plans home, but there may be some ways of thinking worth bringing home from the office. The scrutiny and accountability of business forces individuals to consider their decisions and actions. Impulse and fuzzy thinking are relegated in favour of rationality and justification. It may dampen genius, but it allows companies to function collectively. This kind of accountability is missing when it comes to individual planning. There may be people to whom you must or choose to account for your actions in your personal life, but in the vast majority of cases it is really only up to us, and we would rather not call ourselves to account. Follow your heart if you must, but do it with your eyes open.

Why are otherwise sensible people so bad at planning their lives? Alan Giles has a group of close friends who often meet up for a drink: 'They're all pretty senior, running businesses and so on. The thing is, in terms of personal finance, we're all crap even though we all partly got to where we are by being very rigorous and disciplined at handling corporate funds, investment, and financial planning, yet none of us do it at home. It's not because we don't know how to do it, but maybe it feels too much like the day job.'

This dissonance between work and personal attitudes was wonderfully illustrated in a chat with Carol Rosati, a senior headhunter at Harvey Nash, a global recruitment firm. Businesses come to her to find someone to fill a key role, having given careful thought to the future needs of the organisation and the kind of individual who will be able to fulfil those needs. This might be for a limited time, e.g. a start-up might be looking for someone now at the seed stage who may not be the same person to take the business to £100m. Job applicants, on the other hand, tend not to have a route map for their careers. They are far more focused on the role in front of them, and usually go with gut instinct. So the same high flying individuals who may have sat on the hiring side of the table, who in their business lives would have a ready portfolio of analytical and planning tools to help with business decisions, abandon or forget them when it comes to their own career decisions.

We asked Carol what lies behind this. 'Why don't people plan in personal life? Fear. People are motivated to show they're successful at work and behave accordingly. They think, "If I do x y z, then this will happen". In their personal lives, people just bumble along. They'd rather not face or address difficult issues, financial or personal. That's easier than having difficult conversations.'

Finding a bottom line

Whilst there may be no end of confusion about the vision and the mission statement, the corporate values, social impacts and the brand key/onion/cathedral/tree, lurking underneath in a business there is certainty that money must be made. Maybe not this year, maybe not even next, but amongst all the other uncertainties, making money is what a company is for. Breaking even may be good enough and loss can get carried forward for a while but to continue to exist long-term, a business can't lose more than it spends.

What makes planning so much more difficult for individuals is that we don't have a clear bottom line in the same way. Rather we tend to have vague conceptions of 'happiness' or 'fulfilment', when pressed. We will look at how to deal with this in Chapter 4.

But effective future planning in a business demands clarity beyond just the bottom line. In a world of flux, confusion and possibility, one where a handset manufacturer used to be a paper mill (Nokia) or a US railway manufacturer now runs cinemas (Reading), there is a danger that companies will look to their future and see no limits.

Freed by limits

In the same way that a person can have transferable skills which mean they can jump sectors, companies can identify particular areas of skill and expertise which might be useful in sectors they haven't operated in previously. Retailers, for example, might look at the business and describe their key attributes in a way which opens up future doors beyond the traditional retail sector: customer data analysis experts, logistical wizards, service supremos, localising legends. It is great to be able to feel you have the skills to get you out of a rut. No one wants to be the Blockbuster story, stuck in their past groove as the walls close in on them. However, adding almost infinite possibility to the uncertainty of the future would make for a chaotic and unwieldy strategic plan.

When doing futures planning for a company like (for example) Coca-Cola, looking ten years ahead, it is incredibly useful and (counter-intuitively perhaps) liberating to know that whatever changes might be made to product or service, the company intended to remain a beverage company. Businesses need to be open to possibilities, to appreciate that the make-up of the market may change and that competitors may spring up from surprising sources, but not so flexible that they do not stand for anything. Strategy also has to include what companies (and individuals) will not do.

When you go into a company as a consultant on strategic/scenario planning, it is essential that the participants in the exercise are aware that they are the ones expert in their own company and, in all likelihood, the sector. This insider knowledge is a central part of the process if the exercise is going to be meaningful and useful for the company. Their knowledge is required to determine what the company would or would not do; what it would or would not become in a changing world. That knowledge is also a key source for assessing the significance of different drivers of change for the business, and deciding the strategic response.

The process would run differently with different outcomes if you were doing it with a different group of people. Even within a company, different departments will do it differently even if the question is the same. Similarly, when individuals are doing personal planning, it is something they have to do for themselves. What makes sense for you won't make sense for someone else, and you can't borrow someone else's life plan.

You gotta do it

A full-blown scenario planning exercise can take months, even years. Scenario planning purists would shudder at a compact, zipped version, although I maintain that if you are focused enough you can extract useful elements and turn them to your own ends and timetable. However, there is one way in which the purists are definitely right in focusing on the time and effort invested, and that is the fact that going through the process is often as useful as the final scenarios – sometimes even more so.

For businesses concerned about team building and collaboration, a scenario planning exercise is an incredibly powerful way to get people together. After some initial scratchiness, the team is thinking together, building a common narrative together, and an intellectual openness seems to bring emotional openness with it. At the end, the team has built something which is useful and meaningful for them and the company. The company dinners or drinks which usually follow are, in my experience, exceptionally warm and friendly. A far better return on investment – and fewer bruises – than paintball I reckon.

Commissioning scenario planning is something of a leap of faith. Some clients just 'get it' – maybe they have had a good experience before, or their outlook is such that they are intellectually 'open' to the outside. Even for these converts, however, as the calendar fills it can be tempting to try to skip to the last page. Can they delegate the workshop(s) to other people, and just write an approving introduction to whatever gets produced? Sign off some budget to try and ensure the findings are effectively spread around the organisation?

But by doing this they would be truly missing out. The process of scenario planning requires people to bring to the surface their assumptions about the business, what they think the business does and should do. Very often in an organisation, consensus is wrongly presumed. Going through the possible drivers of change which are having an impact on the organisation forces people to really think about how the sector may be changing. It makes them face up to scary competition and potential disruption which may be far more comfortable, but dangerous, to ignore.

In every exercise there are always some eureka moments: 'I never thought of it that way' or 'That's a really helpful way to look at things'. Similarly for individuals, with all the people who helped out as guinea pigs for this book, they all spontaneously highlighted how much they had learned from just going through the process. More than that, of course, storytelling is an incredibly powerful way to move people to face the future, whether they are at home or at work. 'The best way to get humans to venture into unknown terrain is to make that terrain familiar and desirable by taking them there first in their imaginations[36].'

The power

There is one more relevant lesson to learn from futures planning with businesses. One of the most depressing experiences in this is carrying out exciting, innovative, creative, investigative futures work with a business only to be told at the end that none of the fabulous

---

36   Tichy, Noel. *The Leadership Engine*. New ed. London: HarperCollins, 2002.

strategy and ideas will ever see the light of day. It is really important at the beginning to know what the remit for creating strategy or for implementing change really is. Similarly, unless you just really like the mental gymnastics, when it comes to planning for your own life, you need to have a sense of whether you are actually ready to do anything, to make any changes. Decide against a commitment if you have thought about the outcomes and positively rejected them; don't just walk away because you can't be bothered to think about it.

The ups and downs of being first in class: The great firewall of China

There is a consensus amongst forecasters that by 2020, or even before, China will be the world's largest economy. 18 years ago, however, most Western companies were afraid to do business there. It was widely perceived as an arid economic desert, where the strongest brand was the Communist Party and the government could summarily crush any Western business venture. In 1994, Cisco, the US computer company, established operations in China. To many, it must have looked like corporate insanity. But for over a decade it thrived, and the decision was applauded internationally. How did they do it? It can't have been an unemotional decision. In 1994, Cisco was an all-American company and the people working at Cisco, along with their families, neighbours and the media, had strong feelings about what Cisco was proposing.

Cisco's remarkable success is a testament to the potential pay-offs of futures planning and taking calculated risks on a possible scenario. But in 2012, Cisco's story is also an example of how planning for the future is never a one-off exercise. In recent years, accusations of collusion with the Chinese government to monitor dissidents have plagued the company.

Leaked documents showed that in 2002, Cisco took China's 'Golden Shield' initiative, an online censorship system, and turned it into a business opportunity, selling about $100,000 worth of routers put to use in censorship.[37] In 2011, it was announced that Cisco (among other companies) was helping China to build a video surveillance system on a large scale in the city of Chongqing, potentially sealing the deal by skirting a US ban on selling crime-control equipment to China. The system is intended to allow for multiple uses, 'to tame, say, either traffic jams or democracy marches'.[38] A researcher from Amnesty International reports that 'there's ample evidence' that China uses video surveillance to 'crack down and then criminalise' political activity.[39] Cisco has maintained that it does not tailor its equipment for the Chinese government, but a report from the Human Rights Law Foundation in Washington DC claims that the products were specifically designed to target the Falun Gong, a religious group in China.[40]

Cisco announced it was creating a specific business unit to focus on China in 2010, perhaps in response to the fact that its market share is 'lower in China than in almost any other country'.[41] China is still likely seen as a great opportunity (if somewhat of a liability publicly) for Cisco. Overall, Cisco's stock has been down 'about 40% since April 2010' and its strategy must adapt as its priority markets become emerging markets and its competitive landscape shifts.[42]

---

37 '"Great Firewall" of China Was a Chance to Sell More Routers', *Wired* magazine, 20 May 2008.

38 'Cisco Poised to Help China Build Surveillance Project', *Wall Street Journal*, 5 July 2011

39 *Wall Street Journal*, 5 July 2011.

40 'Group Says It Has Evidence of Cisco's Misdeeds in China', *The New York Times*, 2 September 2011.

41 'Cisco Aims at China Market With Restructuring', *PC World*, 12 January 2010.

42 'Cisco Announce a Three Year Plan – Challenge for Services, China, Cloud and R&D', Phil Hassey, capioIT blog, 16 September 2011.

4

Human Drivers: The Inside Story

'The first principle is that you must not fool yourself –
and you are the easiest person to fool.'
– Richard Feynman, Nobel Prize winner in physics

The grand scheme of things

'No one on their deathbed said they wished they had spent more time in the office.' I can't find the original author, but whoever said it first, this quote sticks around because it resonates so strongly. However pressing that deadline, however big the order, however desired the promotion, we all sense that 'proper perspective' (and we'll look in a moment at what that actually means) makes us realise what is really important. That in the grand scheme of things, when we step back from the pointillist painting of our lives, made up of these dots of actions and little decisions, the broader pattern and direction is what really matters.

When it comes to searching for perspective, it is possible, of course, to zoom too far out. We are all mortal (sorry) and as the universe expands, our place in it gets ever smaller and less important (sorry again). We are nothing. Floating bits of dust, tiny cogs whirring along, making not a blind bit of difference to anything…You do matter, though. A lot. Especially to you (I hope). You should matter to you, and if you don't then please find a professional who can help you.

Existential ants

There are many interesting ways in which philosophers can try to make us understand where we fit in the grand scheme of things. Go to the top of any tall building and look down as the ground recedes. Find one high enough, and soon enough the people below start to look like ants, scurrying around on esoteric missions. In our daily life, the mundane decisions, battles, triumphs and disappointments occupy front of mind, as they should, but some mental space and time should be left to consider the big picture.

Some people find meditation allows daily concerns to find their proper place; others find that physical distance is required to create mental distance. But physical distance alone cannot guarantee perspective. When the illusionist David Blaine shut himself in a plexiglass box suspended over the River Thames for 44 days, he said he wanted to get 'closer to real life'. I always found this very odd, as surely real life was the crowds underneath mischievously cooking burgers to distract him, and endlessly trying to find how he was cheating? I guess, though, that it worked for him, and all of us need some version of that plexiglass box to let us find perspective.

Only human

What drives us? Why do you do what you do? Why did you choose that? Why not the other thing? How should we understand the internal drivers of our behaviour, and where do they fit in the grand scheme of individual future planning?

The best laid plans...

The Internet, TV and bookshelves are full of helpful tips and tricks for how we can improve our lives. With its internal emphasis, self-help tends to focus on showing us how we can unscramble ourselves from the inside out. External stimuli and reality are less important: what really matters is how we internalise these stimuli and therefore how we react emotionally. Hence the focus is on what goes on inside people's heads, and therefore we are offered techniques to show us how to identify how our thought patterns and emotional habits are making us see the outside world and other people in a certain way, and how to change that. Thus we can think ourselves happy/thin/rich/calm/sexy.

Makeover shows have added a whole new dimension to the self-help genre. A charismatic outsider (or team) is brought in to boost self-confidence and rewire the internal dialogue, thus supercharging self-esteem by the end of the show, if not permanently. It's what is on the inside that counts – although this may also come with some helpful external cues like new clothes and make-up or even a new face.

In case you haven't realised it by now, this book makes no claims to be able to reach the inner you (Not saying you aren't fabulous. You are. Really.) Nonetheless, it would be foolish to try to write a book about future planning without addressing the fact that we are all driven to do the things we do and make the choices that we make by a complex variety of factors, including internal ones. Instead, this book is about applying rational logic and some degree of objectivity to questions and problems which affect us on a personal level.

Devilish detail

What drives one person? Can we micro-analyse every decision in a life? Should we even try? Think about your daily routine. Let's start from the beginning. Do you have an alarm clock? What kind? Your phone, perhaps? Why did you choose that alarm sound over another? What do you do when you first hear the sound? Why?

Do your check your e-mails, voicemails or Twitter first? We could go minute by minute through the minutiae of your life and scrutinise the decisions which lie behind your routine, but I've had enough already.

Trying to describe (let alone understand) it all is an impossible task. Unless you have an impressive Narcissus complex or an OCD issue which you need to get to grips with, it rapidly gets quite boring. A constant attempt to rationalise what we have just done, to deconstruct and (hopefully) justify the choice we have made, would drive us mad. We would spend so much time analysing the things we do that we would have no time to do anything else.

The lives we lead are an agglomeration of micro-choices, again like the pointillist painting which only makes sense at a distance. This book is about long-term planning so it makes sense to take a broader view of what drives us, of what drives you. It is not trying to deny the existence of impulse and spontaneity, or aim to get you to post and pre-rationalise your every decision. Rather we have to have a sense of, and take into account, the overarching human drivers which tend to push us in a certain direction.

What's your bottom line?

One of the things which enables companies to plan effectively is a shared, so-damn-obvious-we-don't-have-to-spell-it-out sense of the bottom line. While there may be fuzziness about the vision and arguments about the mission, somewhere behind the CSR concerns sits the certainty that the company has to make more money than it spends. It may be changing from a product to a service company, it may be disaggregating or reaggregating, bringing happiness, solving a global crisis or just providing a tasty beverage, but it has to do this while turning a profit (or at least breaking even) or none of this can happen. And the more money the company makes, the more of this can happen. Profit being secured is the key result, and the rest can follow.

This clarity is extremely helpful, humming and influencing quietly in the background when it comes to comparing and assessing strategic options. The path to profit, the best way to drive down costs and the correct ratio of marketing investment to return may be fiercely contested, but everyone agrees on this basic principle.

However, when it comes to individuals and how we shape our future, we may need to work out what our own bottom line is. We often leave it at a vague sense of 'doing well' or 'being happy', but this can mean very different things to different people. It matters because while we leave it vague at the doing and living stage, the sense that we haven't achieved *whatever it is*, that we are disappointed, that something hasn't quite lived up to expectations is sharp and acute on reflection.

What makes you happy?

Finding out what really makes you happy can be a lifelong task. Some people seem to know intuitively, while others may invest a lot of effort, money and airmiles trying to find out. If people are lucky, they get to the answer before their time is up – or before their idea of happiness changes yet again as they age.

There may be mental and emotional barriers to finding, or feeling, happiness, which require the expertise of a trained psychoanalyst to identify and deal with. It would be a wild and crazy promise to even suggest this book could deal with such issues.

Instead, what I am suggesting is that it's worth being aware of what makes you happy on a basic level, and what makes you feel successful in your life. If you are considering different paths and options for the future, you want to be able to identify which one is actually likely to be the best for you. It requires some distance from the now, and how you feel now (the now is very powerful, I know, I know, nonetheless) and the ability to project how your older self in five or ten or twenty years' time would feel about the outcome. You need some self-knowledge and understanding to be able to work out what the right future for you is.

If you are trying to plan for your long-term future, you are likely asking questions about a future successful career path, fulfilling relationship or effective financial plan etc, but how you define success, fulfilment and effectiveness will be different for you than for someone else. It's amazing how little thought we give to exactly what we mean and how often we bandy around key words without understanding how much their definitions can vary, depending on who you're speaking to. You could start at a really basic level. Could you describe what kind of mood you are in at this particular moment, for example? Do you know why you feel that way?

Regrets, I've had a few...

The Internet is full of end-of-life quotes from the famous (or famously articulate), pointing out the importance of not neglecting what really matters. From Abraham Lincoln's 'it's not the years in your life that count. It's the life in your years', to Steve Jobs' 'We don't get a chance to do that many things, and every one should be really excellent. Because this is our life. Life is brief, and then you die, you know? And we've all chosen to do this with our lives. So it better be damn good. It better be worth it.'[43] So much consensus by so many brilliant dead people suggests there may be something in it.

I did it my way

How can we get to a sensible depth of understanding about what drives us in order to inform individual planning? Hopefully you have some self-knowledge here, some sense of your bottom line. If not, don't panic; there are many different driver models you can choose from to find out.[44] Some of these drivers, especially the more basic ones like food and shelter, are universal. Others vary in terms of how strongly they influence different individuals.

Abraham Maslow's 'hierarchy of needs', beloved by marketers everywhere, may be the most useful starting point here. A brief explanation for any readers who haven't sat through a marketing presentation (where *were* you?): Maslow developed the theories that societies and people progress through a succession of stages, with more complex needs developing as the more basic needs are met. At the bottom of the pyramid hierarchy are basic survival needs such as food and shelter. Next come more complex social needs, such as respect and self-esteem. Finally, at the top is the elusive, paradise state of self-actualisation.

This is the most controversial stage. How do you know if someone is self-actualised or not? It's not really something you shout about, as surely the need to broadcast it suggests that it remains elusive and you are stuck in lower-level status needs. More seriously, it may make more sense to see these stages as running in parallel, with different needs having lesser or greater importance at any one time. What has been so unnerving in the recent financial crisis is the extent to which people who had assumed they had

---

44 For example, try 'Self-determination Theory' (Deci and Ryan, 2000, see
    www.selfdeterminationtheory.org), which proposes three basic psychological needs:
    Autonomy (the sense of volition and freedom over our actions); Competence (the
    feeling that we can do what we want or have to do); Relatedness (the sense of
    belonging and feeling of connectedness to others). If thwarted, performance,
    motivation and well-being are diminished.

moved on from the anxieties of lower-level needs suddenly found themselves confronting basic survival challenges.

As with businesses fire-fighting against imminent closure, individuals who are facing survival challenges often push long-term planning to the back of their minds. Immediate and significant threats do not really allow for clear, calm and objective long-term thinking. As Andy Gilbert points out, if you are full of 'hindering thoughts', you are psychologically in the same kind of state as someone running away from a bear, which is not the best time to sit down and consider your long-term future. Thus, techniques like scenario planning – which can be an excellent process for dealing with important issues – are not something to be done in the immediate aftermath of an extreme event, such as 9/11 or when people are in a panic. As Kotler and Caslione say, at such times 'the immediate job of the business lead is not to discover patterns but to stop the bleeding'.[45]

The kind of scenario-planning techniques outlined in this book require a level of assurance that you will have survived to live out the scenarios in the future. However, this is not to say that long-term planning should concern itself only with the fulfilment of more sophisticated, higher-order needs such as status. If your planning covers your job, your income and where you might live, all of these have a direct impact on your lower-level needs and neglecting them for the future would be foolishly inviting the bears in.

A little bit of existential angst does you good

When we want to summarise who we are to other people or ourselves, we illuminate a particular pattern according to obvious

---

45 *Chaotics*, p. 91.

social rules: What do you do? I'm a teacher. I'm a lawyer. I'm a finance director, not 'I wear clothes', 'I cross roads', 'I drink tea'. Where are you from? London, not 'my mother', 'I've just been in the bathroom', 'Earth'. The right and wrong answers in the examples above are clear. One answer allows the conversation to continue, the other has people sidling off.

But when it gets to fundamental questions about who you are, what you want, what would make you happy and where you want to go with your life, the 'pat' answers can be unhelpful. The key thing is to stop and question, to confront those lazy (albeit understandable) assumptions and shortcuts we make when we talk or think about ourselves.

Surfacing assumptions

At a species level, there are many ways in which people have tried to categorise what drives our behaviour: the search for experience, status, affection, security and reason. Trying to spot the patterns in individual decisions and choices is now big business. It really kicked off with the award for the Nobel Prize in Economics to Daniel Kahneman, the first psychologist to win it, as well as the success of *Freakonomics* and subsequent franchise. Now governments around the world are looking to *Nudge* or *Sway* their constituents towards solutions to their behavioural problems. The idea that one can identify rules governing our superficial irrationality is now accepted wisdom.

Finding a balanced perspective

'People don't like rationality, not when it matters.'
– Daniel Kahneman[46]

Is it possible to gain a sense of perspective on one's own life? To do so, it may require the device of pretending to be someone else, or thinking or writing about yourself from an outside perspective – your report, your epitaph, how your biographer or your grandchildren might describe your life looking back. Stephen R. Covey in *The 7 Habits of Highly Effective People* advocates finding a quiet space to do a visualisation exercise for your own funeral, to imagine how you would like to be described in your different roles (family, friend, worker, community) by people who care about you.

Katerina Gould describes a retrospective exercise she does with a number of her clients, to help them understand what their values are. She gets them to look 10 years or 25 years into the future, or into retirement and to think about themselves then without worrying about how they will get there. It allows clients to become much clearer about what is important to them, and help drive decisions about what to do next. Visualising a destination first – one that is not dependent on a path – allows for an injection of creativity and imagination, as well as clarity on goals.

You need to identify what drives you. What would constitute for you a life well-lived: Security? Risk? Family bonds? External approval? When you are framing the questions for your future, these drivers must underlie the frameworks.

---

46   In conversation with the author.

Family matters

The prevailing ethos seems to be that family and affective bonds are what really matter to most people. When the chips are down and the clichés come home to roost, most people, especially the rich and the ill, seem to broadly concur that money can't buy you love, and love is all you need. Managing to create a loving, supportive family environment is a goal for many people. Research around Europe and beyond suggests that, paradoxically, the more unlikely it is that people will achieve the 'perfect family', the more they yearn for it.

Nonetheless, there's no point in planning to create a future which puts family at its centre if you can honestly say that you will feel you have failed in life if you haven't made it to Vice President by the time you are 35. These goals can shift in importance with age and changing circumstances, but long-term planning is about taking into account how your priorities are likely to change while appreciating what is driving you *now*.

Furthermore, while this chapter is about human, internal drivers, the thrust of the book is about the importance of being aware of external realities, and factoring them into your future plans. This is one of the reasons why I think traditional self-help is incomplete by focusing only on the internal offers an incomplete picture.

Take marriage, for example. You are not a statistic and hopefully your (next) relationship will blossom and endure. Nonetheless, the external statistics are not encouraging and depending on where you live, between a third and a half of those who say 'I do' actually won't. Identify and appreciate the depth of your desires, but place them rationally in the external world in which you live. This is not about trying to destroy love's young (old) dream. Rather, a sensible appreciation of the contemporary, external pressures on a relationship is only likely to make it stronger.

You're only human

Behavioural economics is now big business, and big book business. Like the bit at the end of every Scooby-Doo cartoon when the villain turns out to have been someone they all knew, the first eureka moment of behavioural economics for many seems to have been the point when 'Homo Economicus', supposedly rational economic man, was first unmasked as an irrational, impulsive consumer just like the rest of us. While anyone who has ever done any shopping could have told you that people don't always make the most sensible consumption choices, revealing humans as creatures who don't repetitively apply detailed cost–benefit analyses to every decision seems to have a been a bit of a shock to the systems. Now the tables have turned to the point where stock market traders are looking to mine the humanistic depths of social media for use in their own forecasts.

I'm sure part of the appeal behind the popular interest in behavioural economics is that it allows all of us to recognise the patterns in our irrational behaviour, and to realise that our idiosyncratic impulses are not so unique after all. It talks about other people, but helps us learn about us. Yet few of the books go on to suggest ways we might improve our own lives through their analysis. Planning for the future makes so much sense, yet why do we tend to give it so little of our time and attention? It's worth flagging up the common factors which can derail the best laid plans, and which make all of us only human after all:

The triumph of hedonics (or short-term gratification)

Most, if not all, lifestyle diseases come upon us gradually, even if awareness of their presence is a switch which suddenly goes on after a depressing visit to the doctor. You do not become obese overnight – go to bed normal weight, wake up twice the size. Rather, unless genetics are really against you, obesity is a slow, gradual shift to the bigger side, the cumulative effect of thousands of poor short-term decisions. On their own, none of these would add up to obesity, but together the impact is huge.

Who hasn't accepted a slice of cake, had one more glass of wine or ordered chips on the side when they knew they shouldn't? Just one more won't make a difference in the long run. There is a reason one of the classic techniques to try to help people achieve lifestyle change is by focusing on the long-term goal at the moment of temptation. It is much easier to focus on the now and deliberately push away concerns about the long-term impacts, though they often remain at a low-level hum, diminishing the enjoyment of the moment and biting us later as guilt and promises to do better.

In so many things, it is easier to have a short-term focus and ignore the longer term. But no one, (aside from perhaps your parents), is likely to be thinking about this for you. Thinking about the longer-term, about your future, is a positive mental habit that you can develop, and this book can help the habit take hold.

They made me do it

And it is not just you who may be driving you slowly but surely off the straight and narrow. Drs James H. Fowler and Nicholas A. Christakis used the detailed data collected for a study into heart disease over a 60 year period in Framingham, a small community in Massachusetts, to show how behaviours like smoking and obesity can spread through a network in a way usually associated with viral disease. The depth and diffusion of social connections means these effects can spread from people you don't even know. As they describe it in their book, *Connected*, this means that if your friend's friend's friend put on weight, stopped smoking or became happy you would too (or at least would be more likely to). They came up with the ' "three degrees of influence" rule about human behavior: We are tied not just to those around us, but to others in a web that stretches farther than we know'.

Drs Fowler and Christakis identify two key elements of networks: the connections within them, and what they call 'contagion, which pertains to what, if anything, flows across the ties. It could be buckets of water, of course [being passed along a human chain to put out a fire], but it could also be germs, money, violence, fashion, kidneys, happiness or obesity'.[47] They advocate seeing ourselves as part of a 'human superorganism', using the same kind of mental maps as we do for the Internet or our social media networks.

Connected focuses on the network, but the authors also acknowledge the many other factors which can influence personal outcomes such as material wealth, skills and so on. So you can't blame everything bad on other people you don't even know, although they may have had something of a hand in it. According to *Time* Magazine, in 2009 Dr Christakis was named one of the 100 most influential people in the world. I'm not quite sure what this means, but it sounds like he may have been influencing all of us personally. So if you are looking to blame someone for something, whatever it is, maybe try pinning it on him.

---

47   Christakis, Christopher and James Fowler. *Connected: The Amazing Power of Social Networks and How They Shape Our Lives.* London: HarperPress, 2011.

'Unfreedom' of choice

'The odds of going to the store for a loaf of bread and coming out with only a loaf of bread are three billion to one.'
– Erma Bombeck

We are surrounded by choice and temptation. Alvin Toffler first referred to the idea of 'unfreedom' of choice in the 1970s in his book *Future Shock*. The idea, much expanded on since, is that industrial society gives consumers far too many choices on a daily basis, to the point where we can become paralysed by the frequency and complexity of even mundane decisions. Much of the work focuses on consumption choices and the bewildering array of purchase possibilities – 58 types of jam, 500 types of shampoo and so on. One of the interesting typologies divides people into two types, maximisers and satisficers[48], the former agonising over every decision, no matter how small, and always anxious that they have failed to make the best decision. Satisficers, on the other hand, just make decisions on the fly, sometimes at a high ultimate cost to themselves.

As social rules shift and traditional rules and structures break down (see Chapter 5), we also face a bewildering array of choices in our personal lives. In his book *Liquid Love*[49], the eloquent sociologist Zygmunt Bauman talks of a modern setting where ' "romantic possibilities" (and not only "romantic" ones) are supposed and hoped to come and go with ever greater speed and in never thinning

---

48   The idea of satisficing was put forth by the social scientist Herbert Simon in
.   'A Behavioral Model of Rational Choice', in the *Quarterly Journal of Economics*, originally published in 1955. Barry Schwartz develops the idea of maximisers and satisficers in his book, *The Paradox of Choice: Why More is Less* (HarperCollins, 2005).
49   Bauman, Zygmunt. *Liquid Love: On the Frailty of Human Bonds*. Cambridge: Polity Press, 2003.

crowds, stampeding each other off the stage and out-shouting each other with promises to be 'more satisfying and fulfilling'.

For many, choice avoidance may be the easiest way out. Even with the best laid plans, we are vulnerable to negative influence and distraction from ourselves, from others and from outside, sometimes visible, sometimes more insidious. The best we can do is try to raise our awareness of how we operate and how to stay focused. Again, no one is going to make deliberate, conscious choices for your life except you. Hopefully this book might encourage you to face them head on.

5
External Factors

*'Is there not a movement, however tortuous, from ignorance
to knowledge, from mythical thought and childish fantasies to
perception of reality face to face, to knowledge of true goals,
true values as well as truths of fact? Can history be a mere
purposeless succession of events, caused by a mixture of
material factors and the play of random selection, a tale full of
sound and fury signifying nothing? This was unthinkable.
The day would dawn when men and women would take their
lives in their own hands and not be self-seeking beings or the
playthings of blind forces that they did not understand.
It was, at the very least, not impossible to conceive that such
an earthly paradise could be; and if conceivable we could,
at any rate, try to march towards it.'*
– Isaiah Berlin *(The Crooked Timber of Humanity:
Chapters in the History of Ideas)*

The previous chapter was about human drivers, the internal,
individual elements which shape who you are and the direction
you want to go in. However, we all live in this world and external
changes will also have an impact on you and your options. Only
a very small number of people are insulated from what is going
on outside.

Bringing the outside in

'If we can't alter the tide of events,
at least we can be nearby with towels to mop up.'
– Peter David (Q-In-Law
(*Star Trek: The Next Generation*, #18))

Even if the major global shifts in world politics remain at a distance, there are many ways in which macro-economic changes will affect your financial situation, your pension (if you have one), your rent or your mortgage, your salary and your savings. Geopolitics will affect food sources and prices, what is in the shops and where you go on holiday. Environmental drivers may affect many of your consumption choices. Technological advances will continue to affect your lifestyle and your relationship options. New ways of maintaining social networks will allow new ways to keep your social life going. Developments in healthcare could have an enormous impact on your life. Social shifts may alter the possibilities open to you in your personal life, and the censure or encouragement you get from those around you for your personal choices. It is important to remember that no man (or woman) is an island and even when we try to make the most personal of decisions or choices, they represent just one way in which the future is shaped. Whether we like it or not, these external factors will also play a part.

I've worked on projects for a number of large FMCG companies (fast-moving consumer goods, or CPG, consumer packaged goods, companies which sell food and drink and 'home and personal care' – ie toiletries and house cleaning), many of which dedicate whole teams to tracking and anticipating what's going on in the outside world. It is not just global companies, though, which need to look beyond their own borders. All companies could benefit from a broader awareness of change around them. External factors will at the very least have bearing on manufacturing processes, the supply chain, technical efficiencies, product and information flow, to say nothing of their competitive set and consumer demand, to name just a few.

Companies who ignore what is going on outside do so at their peril. Even since I began my consulting career 15 years ago, it is noticeable how many more companies are taking notice of what is going on outside their sector, drafting in increasingly specialised experts in marketing and insight to cover their blind spots in an attempt to predict and prepare and plan for changes even before they happen. There is a growing awareness that in a rapidly evolving world, threats and opportunities can materialise from surprising directions at incredible speeds, and businesses cannot take their own survival for granted. The average lifespan of a company listed in the S&P 500 index of leading US companies has decreased by more than 50 years in the last century, from 67 years in the 1920s to just 15 years today. According to Yale's Professor Richard Foster, by 2020 more than three-quarters of the S&P 500 will be companies that we have not heard of yet[50]. This alone shows the rate of change in the current market, a rate of change which is more likely to accelerate than slow.

In their book *Peripheral Vision: Detecting the Weak Signals That Will Make or Break Your Company*[51], George S. Day and Paul J. H. Schoemaker say that greatest dangers to companies 'are the ones you don't see coming, and understanding these threats – and

---

50   Professor Richard Foster from Yale University, quoted on BBC website.
51   Day, George S. and Paul J. H. Schoemaker. *Peripheral Vision: Detecting the Weak Signals That Will Make or Break Your Company*. Harvard Business School Press: Cambridge, Massachusetts, 2006.

anticipating opportunities – requires strong peripheral vision'. They illustrate this with the example of Mattel (*Barbie*) and MGA Entertainment (*Bratz*). Perfectly groomed queen *Barbie* completely failed to anticipate that a bunch of streetwise (some say tarty, others say much worse) upstarts might topple her off her pony. By 2006, Bratz had captured about 40% of the fashion-doll market[52] a mere five years after their launch.

CSR and the broader environment

This broader focus on the outside world is not just a product of smart foresight. The growing emphasis on corporate social responsibility and enhanced awareness of a company's role in, and responsibilities towards, its broader environment has also played a part in shifting and expanding horizons. The new focus on ethical trading and corporate transparency means the spotlight may fall on any and every stage in the supply chain, from field to factory to transport to retail to consumption to product disposal. More than simple scrutiny, new technology and consumer interest (albeit a dilettante one) means there is no section of the supply chain which might not be visible and, even, outsourced to consumers. In this age of entrepreneurship, all the following options are open at the time of writing: make your own and sell it on Etsy.com; they make it you sell it, through the Avon cosmetics network; design something and have those clever folk at ponoko. com make it up for you; want to fund a creative project? Go to kickstarter.com and become a patron of the arts. Or just go make your own content and put it on YouTube.

---

52   'Barbie vs. Bratz: It's a Doll-Eat-Doll World', *Time* Magazine, 22 April 2011.

The big reveal

Where businesses used to be able to imagine themselves at the centre of the consumer universe and thus limit their horizons, there has been something of a Copernican shift. Deregulation and disintermediation helped lift the curtain on how businesses work, and allowed consumers access to an understanding of the corporate machine. Soon, day traders found they were able to beat the markets too, much like the professionals. Whether you see it as the professionalisation of consumers, or the amateurisation of business, suddenly the doors of the corporate world have been prised open. Businesses are left circling anxiously, whilst consumers entrench themselves at the centre of the brand and even the supply system. Until recently, entrepreneurship was a postgraduate field of study. Now it is a popular field for undergraduates, and more people are creating viable businesses at an ever younger age.

The change is most visible if you look at the marketing industry. Marketing has undergone nothing less than a revolution over the last 50 years. In the beginning, the job was simply, if somewhat optimistically: *build it and they will come*. As markets became more competitive, the focus shifted towards consumers, and marketing started to move towards identifying people who might need something. Then on to persuading them why they needed it. Then why they wanted it.

It has evolved again since this first revelation. Now we live in a world where social media increasingly runs the show. A whole new set of norms and rules is being forged for brand-consumer interaction, with sometimes painful consequences for those brands who fail to take note. Still reeling from the news that they may not be able to control the brand once it is let loose into the World Wild Web, now brand and marketing directors are having to deal with a further demotion, watching the stage of consumer social media interaction from the stalls, where they sit, hopefully, trying really hard to 'make friends' without stalking.

So what does this mean for businesses in general? Businesses must look beyond their own backyards. Insularity is tantamount to suicide.

However, it should not only be motivated by fear. There is as much carrot as stick. Looking outside has benefits beyond assuaging fears about missing out. 'Thinking out of the box' has become something of a derided management cliché, but addressing the new and the unfamiliar forces people to frame questions differently, and by framing questions differently they will also start to see the world a little differently, and, by necessity, somewhat creatively. Corporate individuals have to go beyond their linguistic (and theoretical) comfort zone of market share or Key Performance Indicators if they are going to get to grips with unfamiliar political or social issues, unfamiliar at least in a business context.

Similarly, for individuals, the mere act of asking themselves new questions – let alone trying to answer them – can open them up to new ways of thinking. This was something the life coaches we interviewed confirmed. As Katerina Gould pointed out, 'using the language of openness and possibility frees people up to be more creative and to not just think linearly'[53].

Where to Look?
PESTO

Businesses and brands have to look outside themselves because that is where the action is. PESTO is not a random reference to

---

53   In conversation with the author.

Italian food but an acronym for one of the ways in which companies traditionally identify and organise the external factors which they need to consider for their future planning: political, economic, social, technological and organisational. Sometimes PEST is enough, other times environmental is added to make STEEP, and sometimes a C for commercial finds its way somewhere into the list.

At first it can seem like a bit of a stretch, but it soon becomes apparent how these broader factors (sometimes described as macro factors) could have a significant impact on a business. Take a food manufacturer, for example: political attitudes towards, and policy around, nutrition and obesity could have a significant impact on where the food is sold and how it is labelled and marketed. Geopolitical factors could affect the supply and cost of ingredients and manufacturing processes. Economic shifts could influence market price sensitivity, manufacturing and wage costs, trade and international sources of competition. Social change will impact the nature of demand and marketing. Technological evolution could impact everything from logistics to retail to consumer access, and so on.

As individuals, we can also see a connection, albeit an indirect one, between these macro factors and our own lives. Let's say, for example, you're considering relocating for work to another country. Economic factors might increase political pressure to restrict immigration, leading to tighter visa restrictions and fewer job opportunities or companies willing to sponsor visas. Additionally, social changes in attitude may have an impact on approval and acceptance of your domestic arrangements: will you be shunned if you are unmarried but living together, will your unusual clothing choices limit your, or your child's, social circle? Technological changes will impact how you maintain remote relationships and connect locally. Environmental factors may impact your appetite for and ease of travel.

Sometimes links between macro factors and our lives are explicit – policy diktats on the number of children in China, say. In the economic sphere we have all become somewhat fluent, or at least aware, of the way in which the broader economic climate can affect unemployment, interest rates, the availability of credit and the risks of house buying. Oil prices can have a clear impact on the cost of transport, and a less clear one on the cost of plastic manufacture and therefore the prices of common household purchases.

Thinking in this way may be difficult at first but the more you do it, the easier it becomes. By engaging with certain macro-scale issues we become, as Dr Philipp Rode put it: 'somewhat a strategic animal. There's a learning opportunity where it's not directly about the content, but about the more general logic with which you engage. Breaking [the future] down into digestible pieces at the individual level, I would consider that a rather healthy process of thinking.'[54]

There are a couple of points to note about Figure 1 (see overleaf):

1. Many macro factors that can be defined as 'political' are largely manifested as economic to the individual – tax rates, incentives for small business, etc.

2. As the digital and the real worlds converge, having technology as a separate driver makes less and less sense.

---

54 In conversation with the author.

Driver	Example	Impacts	Personal Impact Areas
P - Political	1. Support/legislation for small businesses 2. Political attitudes to abortion	1. Would impact your appetite or requirement for private education, healthcare, etc. 2. Accessibility of abortions	1. Career 2. Health, career
E - Economic	1. Interest rates 2. Availability and quality of state-funded health, education and welfare	1. Personal saving/spending, availability of credit 2. Impact the entrepreneurial environment, possibility of setting up own business	1. Financial investment, home ownership 2. Education, Healthcare, Career
S - Social	1. Acceptability of non-married or single parent families 2. Demographic shift to increased proportion of older people	1. Family structure 2. Changing behaviour of older people and attitudes towards ageing and youthfulness	1. Having children 2. Having children, career, health, financial investments, relationships
T - Technological	1. Technological advancements	1. Cost and availability of video calling impacting how you can maintain relationships. Extent to which you need to retrain to maintain job	1. Relationships, career, education

Figure 1: Examples of how macro factors impact on personal life

It matters

Somewhere between the macro and the micro factors sit the thorny issues which, whether we like it or not, can affect how we navigate the world. This is the room where the elephants of racism, sexism and ageism sit, quiet hopefully most of the time, but at times powerful. The unchangeables (pretty much) of your birth may make your chosen path more of an uphill struggle. They are surmountable, we hope, but it would be foolish to suggest all these shadows have vanished simply as a function of other change.

The end of certainty

In this era of dizzying change, both companies and individuals need to look around and outside. They need to consider what is possible and what is probable, as well as recognise knowledge gaps and try to fill them, from the known unknowns to the unknown ones. No job is safe from hot-desking and portfolio career-carving is becoming something of a survival skill. If looking outside gives you vertigo, there's all the more reason to keep doing it until you acclimatise. Panic-inducing articles in management magazines describe a world where only the most agile will survive, accumulating transferable skills to apply to whatever opportunity the world throws at them. Find the Darwinian analogies unpalatable? Then see it instead as a game of musical chairs – the world is shifting beneath you and there will be a scramble for space, for resource, for attention – and have an eye to where you could be when the music stops.

Patterns in the chaos

> *'History is the fiction we invent to persuade ourselves that*
> *events are knowable and that life has order and direction.'*[55]
> – Calvin and Hobbes

Like Calvin, Nassim Taleb has also expertly analysed what he terms the 'narrative fallacy', 'our tendency to perceive – to impose – narrativity and causality'[56]. Although ambiguity is difficult for people to deal with, fear about the future can be mitigated by taking into account those things which humans can process, account and plan for. While the arguments in *Black Swan* do a good job of pointing out the limitations of assigning scientific value to a narrative that may gloss over key factors, it is worth reminding ourselves that this phenomenon is so ubiquitous because we will try to make a connection, we will try to find the story. A narrative, however flawed, may be more useful than none at all. Something will fill the gap, and some simplification is necessary for people to be able to take a long view.

Looking outside, being able to discern a pattern and see how broader elements can impact on your own life can be a way to calm the chaos and to create a foothold, a sense of stability in dizzying change. In the way that dancers are trained to keep their eye on a fixed point of distance when they spin in order to avoid dizziness, it is worth lifting your focus above the melee of confusion and uncertainty right in front of you to see what is indeed the bigger picture, and then look back down to

---

55 Watterson, Bill. *Homicidal Psycho Jungle Cat*. London: Sphere, 1995.
56 Taleb, Nassim Nicholas. *Black Swan: The Impact of the Highly Probable*. New ed. London: Penguin, 2008.

perceive your place within it and the directions in which you could go.

Beset by change and disruption, some of which will be momentous, some of which will pass with barely a ripple, how can we tell what will be important? As Andy Grove, former Intel CEO, puts it: 'Signal or noise?...Think of the change in your environment, technological or otherwise, as a blip on your radar screen. You can't tell what that blip represents at first but you keep watching radar scan after radar scan, looking to see if the object is approaching, what its speed is and what shape it takes as it comes closer. Even if it lingers on your periphery, you will keep an eye on it because its course and speed may change.'[57] The simple answer? Think it through, keep watching and evaluating, and it gets easier with practice.

Knowing your boundaries

Almost as important as having an open mindset is knowing what factors you do not need to include as you build a picture of the future. Without this filter, you could find yourself speculating to infinity. Beyond common sense, there are no hard and fast rules here. We need to keep reminding ourselves that we are seeking to identify drivers which will be useful and meaningful to us in answering a particular question about the future. There must always be a clear and sensible logic – potentially explicable to someone else not just to you – as to how and why this driver impacts your question.

---

57   Grove, Andrew S. *Only the Paranoid Survive*. New York: Doubleday, 1996.

Wildcards

'What's the worst that can happen?
A tidal wave? Glaciers with guns?'
– Stephen Colbert[58]

PESTO-type models make assumptions of probable and therefore somewhat predictable patterns. However, history would have taught us nothing if not to expect the unexpected. Formal future planning processes such as scenario planning also try to take into account what are known as 'wildcards', those far-out, highly improbable things which, if they *did* occur, would have a huge impact on the outcome.

'A New Species of Trouble'[59]

The delineation of what wildcards should be taken into account changes with time, as events and disruptions force us to face new possibilities. The events of 9/11, for example, made the idea of potential terrorist attack or sabotage on a business, with dramatic effect on supply or logistics, a sensible wildcard to include in future planning. Some wildcards are so dramatic that inclusion becomes pointless. An asteroid hitting and destroying Earth, for example, is not worth factoring in as the impact is such only Hollywood can suggest it is worth crafting a strategic response.

Distillation

We will look in a bit more detail in Chapter 7 in the 'Systems thinking' section on coping with multiple variables. What is likely, regardless of which type of future planning you are doing, is that at

58   Stephen Colbert, Twitter, 11 May 2009.
59   Slovic, Paul. 'Terrorism as Hazard: A New Species of Trouble', *Risk Analysis*,
      22: 425–426, 2002

some point you will want to simplify your model and narrow down the list of factors you are dealing with. One way to do this is by identifying the 'dependencies'. This means illuminating which factors are largely dependent on others so you can simplify your model to just include the base factors on which others depend.

Let's say, a luxury chocolate manufacturer has identified three separate drivers which would impact the question on the future of their industry: retail rents, consumer disposable income and economic growth. Both retail rents and consumer disposable income depend on economic growth rates sufficiently to be able to simplify the drivers just to economic growth in the model. It is noticeable, and perhaps not surprising, how often economic factors emerge as one of the significant base drivers of so much of company planning. This is also the case for individual planning, as we will see shortly. Money does indeed make the world go round.

Where you meet the world
In control?

'I can levitate birds. No one cares.'
– Woody Allen

As first raised on p. 29, one of the critical things to understand when you are identifying and analysing macro or external factors is working out what – if anything – you can control. We are all guilty at times of feeling we have a sense of control when we don't, of superstitiously crediting our action as the trigger for an unrelated outcome, of believing that by gripping on to the arm rests of the plane as tightly as possible we are helping to hold it up.

The extent to which we believe we have control over events which affect us is expressed in psychology by the theory of the 'locus of control'[60]. This can be 'internal' – a belief that the person controls the world around them – or 'external' – the opposite belief that the world around them is controlled by the environment, other people or a higher power. Where you are on the scale will determine to what extent in general you feel you have control over your fate. The psychology rapidly becomes very complicated, as some internally generated factors (such as fear of flying) may be perceived as external and vice versa, confusion as to where to place 'luck' etc, but the key idea to hold on to here is that the extent to which you have control over the world around you has a significant subjective element.

When you do future planning in business, at least at the initial phase of 'futurescaping', of considering the future landscape and drivers of change, you deliberately take the business out of the equation. This is somewhat artificial. If you are considering the future of food retail for the country's biggest supermarket, for example, then the supermarket itself could have an enormous impact on what stores look like, what they sell and even what consumers will demand. However, in order to be able to work through the process without tying the brain into knots, initially you imagine and project the landscape as it would be without the particular intervention of this business, and only later consider what they themselves could impact, what change they could drive, when you are crafting strategy, the strategic *response* to future change.

In individual planning, we are ultimately looking at an individual, at the micro level of change and impact. As we will see in Chapter 8, taking ourselves completely out of the picture as an agent of change would result in a general portrait of the future which may

---

60   Developed by Julian B. Rotter in 1954, then expanded. See also 'An Examination of the Relationship among Career Decision-Making Self-Efficacy, Career Salience, Locus of Control and Vocational Indecision,' Karen M. Taylor and Joellen Popma, *Journal of Vocational Behavior*, 37, 17-31 (1990).

be all very nice but not so helpful as an instrument of individual decision-making. For this reason, we accept the centrality of people in their own lives and make one of the axes the decision itself, the thing over which the individual has complete control.

It's all me

The philosophy of 'personal empowerment' is a staple of self-help. At its best, it enables people who feel at the painful mercy of the world around them to correctly identify the areas where they can make a behavioural or attitudinal change which will lead to a clear improvement in their life. To put it another way, there are strategies to enable you to become more 'internal' on the locus of control spectrum mentioned above. Some of these can be very helpful.

In *The 7 Habits of Highly Effective People*, Stephen R. Covey suggests looking at the language you use to identify (and therefore change) how you deal with the world. He advocates a shift from reactive to proactive language:[61]

Reactive Language	Proactive Language
There's nothing I can do	Let's look at our alternatives
That's just the way I am	I can choose a different approach
He makes me so mad	I control my own feelings
They won't allow that	I can create an effective presentation
I have to do that	I will choose an appropriate response
I can't	I choose
I must	I prefer
If only	I will

Figure 2

---

61 Covey, Stephen R. *The 7 Habits of Highly Effective People*. Reprint edition. London: Simon & Schuster, 2004.

However, at its worst the philosophy of personal empowerment can promise a delusional level of control over the world around you, resulting in disappointment and distracting you from focusing on things where you could in fact make some positive change. Chanting your power will not unblock the sink. There is also a more insidious message, an insinuation of blame which sometimes creeps in: if you can change anything because you have sufficient desire or will to do so, if you have failed to make whatever these changes are (regardless of whether they are really within your locus of control) then the implication is that the fault lies with you for not wishing hard enough. There: *the secret's* out.

Rules of control
Work it out

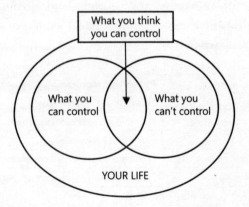

What you think you can control

What you can control

What you can't control

YOUR LIFE

Figure 3

Can we come up with a watertight theory for individual future planning to categorise those things which are within and outside of your control? For every rule, there are many exceptions: career path, relationships, community development and so on. How, on the one hand, can we try to make sure that we are sufficiently aware of our own power to change things to make a difference to our world without wasting energy on pointlessly tilting at windmills, or arranging deckchairs on the Titanic? (Unless deckchair arrangement is your job, in which case we applaud your dedication.) You have to take a rational stance and think it through.

Desperate heroism, battling to victory (ideally) against the odds is a staple of popular culture, from the Battle of Thermopylae (the inspiration for the film *300*) to Marvel Comic superheroes to Hollywood films based on real-life stands made against corporate titans (e.g. *Erin Brockovich, Philadelphia*) to the latest Muppets movie. How can you sensibly assess whether something falls within your locus of control or if you are condemned to a no-hope stand? By understanding the process by which change occurs in each particular sphere. If you're railing against politics, you need to understand the political system in order to see how you might effect change. Erin Brockovich had to become a legal expert, the comic superheroes have to first understand their enemies to beat them, and the Muppets had to remember it is all about show business.

6

Getting Objective

Objectivity-Is-Us

This book is based on the idea that becoming more objective about our lives when it comes to key decisions will allow us to make better judgements. 'Better' because being a bit less subjective allows us to clear some of the emotional haze and fear which surround big decisions, so we can give correct weight to all the things that will impact, and be impacted by, that same decision.

Nobody sees the world quite like you do, and nobody experiences *your* world in the same way. Even at the most basic level, our sensory perception of the world is highly personal and subject to distortions. If you do a Google image search for 'sensory homunculous', you will find a figure of the human body where the proportions of body parts are sized based on the amount of nerves in them. The hands and lips are enormous, dwarfing the rest of the body. It's a fascinating (if somewhat grotesque) illustration of how reality can be represented in different ways. When it comes to our own lives, to managing and prioritising the events and joys and slights that face us, we can assume that we all experience and see them in a slightly different way.

There is a variety of handy management tools out there to help us shrink the obstacles which our own perception puts in our way. Want to work more productively with your colleagues? Try the 'Enneagram of Personality' model. It can place you and your colleagues into one of nine personality types, illuminating what drives you, what you fear, what you desire, your virtues and vices, and how therefore you can all best get on. (I participated in an Enneagram session once. It didn't quite deliver on the promised improvement on workplace dynamics. What it did do very effectively was reinforce and justify why all of us Number Sevens – Role: Enthusiasts; Ego Fixation: Planning; Temptation: Thinking fulfilment was somewhere else – couldn't cope with the Number Eights – Role: Challenger; Ego Fixation: Vengeance; Temptation: Thinking they are completely self-sufficient. Impossible to work with, right?)

The 'Eisenhower Matrix', a prioritising method named after the US President who allegedly invented it, can help us distinguish what is urgent from what is important: urgent and important? Do it immediately. Not important, not urgent? Do it later. Urgent but not important? Delegate it to someone else. Or we can turn to Victor H. Vroom[62], a Professor at Yale, who has created the Vroom–Yetton decision model to help us work out what kind of leadership style is best suited to a particular situation.

All of these models are an attempt to corral subjectivity and emotions which may confuse us via the use of a formula which forces some degree of objectivity. It is clearly an area where people need help.

> The 4-box matrix is perhaps the most beloved corporate/management device. There is nothing which can't be made to look more logical and meaningful by putting it into the 2x2 box format. Give it a go: put labels of 'Carbs' and 'Coffee' at the top and 'Breakfast' and 'Lunch' down the side. Now fill in some ticks and crosses in the boxes. You see? This is now The Meal Record. The Carbinator. Everything looks more impressive. In the case of futurescaping, however, there's a point.

---

62   This really is his name.

Talking to life and executive coaches was an important part of research for this book. These are experts who not only confront professional issues every day, but have to prescribe ways to resolve them. All the coaches we interviewed stressed the importance of objectivity as a tool for self-awareness and, thus, self-improvement. As Katerina Gould, founder of Thinking Potential, pointed out: 'having an objective view of your situation gives you freedom from fixed and repetitive thought patterns. Most people find it difficult to be objective so they need some freedom to create that space, or a person to help them do it, without judgement.' Lauren Zander, the chairman of the Handel Group, an executive coaching and personal life coaching company based in New York City, who teaches a course called 'Designing your Life' at MIT, says what she finds 'to be the most dysfunctional part of someone's life is that they don't tell a fair story. They only tell a story from their point of view...One of the first things I have clients do is analyse themselves so someone else can see it'.

Objectivity can enable us to circumvent the false barriers around our horizons and abilities. A key component of self-awareness is a sense of how you impact others and how others see you, which may be far better than you see yourself, or not, but is likely to be different. Getting someone else to help can be really useful. At the very least they can keep asking you 'why?' or 'why not?' when you describe things you can or cannot, should or should not do, to see where on earth you got that idea from.

Get real!

> *'The friend is the man who knows all about you,*
> *and still likes you.'*
> – Elbert Hubbard

Being objective can be painful. Other people's perspective can jar with the pictures we have built up of ourselves. Nothing quite matches that sinking feeling when a friend playfully shows their phone video of your coolly ironic dance moves from the end of the party, magnified by the fear that this may be how you will be remembered forever.

Dreams, grand aspirations and fantasies of a fabulous future can have a powerful place in helping people get through their lives and indeed better them. However, there is a point when hope becomes delusion and a sustaining fantasy becomes a resource-sapping diversion. This is not a popular message – it goes against a powerful meme around the importance of shoring up self-esteem, and the empowerment message of popular self-improvement insists that one should see no limits on one's potential – and anyone who does is pointlessly and negatively limiting their options.

It presents an interesting ethical/existential dilemma: is it better to spend one's entire life wrongly believing that one is especially talented, or better to have a more balanced view of one's own abilities? Delusional happiness or truth? This is a question only you can answer for yourself. Some people would prefer to know their moonwalk looks like they've had an embarrassing wardrobe malfunction, and are trying to shuffle off the dance floor as quickly as possible. Others just want to enjoy the music.

I know you are a fabulous dancer, though. Really, you're amazing. There may be some areas of your life where you really don't want or demand an objective point of view, and would rather bask in blissful subjective ignorance. Nonetheless, unless you are the most balanced, self-aware person (or, conversely, couldn't care less about anything at all), there will be areas of your life where a non-subjective perspective could be very helpful indeed.

How to get objective?
Go away

Being too objective can make you ill. Or at least, there is a recognised disorder known as Depersonalisation Disorder, a syndrome where people feel too distanced from themselves, detached from their body and mental processes. However, for most people, achieving any sense of objectivity on their life and issues requires effort. Often, physical distance from the place of challenge or anxiety can help us 'find perspective' – going to another room, stopping what one is doing or even just sitting down and having a nice cup of tea to collect your thoughts and be able to put them aside temporarily. It is this dynamic of distance bestowing perspective which leads to the paradoxical impetus to go to faraway places to 'find oneself'.

For most of us, most of the time, an exotic retreat to 'get away from it all' is an unattainable luxury. How can we find objectivity while still living our daily lives, going through our daily routines, as ourselves? One way is to deliberately break with routine – find somewhere new, a different coffee shop, or even just a different seat in the same coffee shop. If you want to get some perspective on something in your home life, try not to do the thinking when you are sitting in bed in your pyjamas or at the kitchen table, if that is your default home location. If you want to stay in the house, then at least sit in a chair you don't normally sit in. Likewise, if you're facing a work decision, don't try to resolve it in the office; instead tackle it at home or, even better, somewhere neutral.

Pretend you are someone else describing you in the third person –a 'school report' of yourself. Imagine you are a coach advising you. What might the coach say? Imagine you are yourself 30 years from now looking back. How might you see things then?

Temporal distance, or planning for a distant future, can also help. In the same way the longer-term future planning in companies allows the participants to leave behind their own personal concerns about career and performance and focus on the greater good of the business, thinking about a distant future for yourself can free you from obsessing about the daily concerns and niggles which tint your everyday perspective. In five or ten years' time, these things will somehow have been resolved – I will have given up smoking, the car door will either work or have been replaced (car or door), the dog will either be better or, um, dead.

The secret formula

Processes like the one outlined in this book can also assist in achieving a measure of objectivity by reframing the familiar in unfamiliar ways. They force you to re-consider and re-define yourself and your life. This enables a shift away from the old grooves and ways of seeing. Doing a version of scenario planning on your own life (see Chapter 8) can enable you to tell a story about your own future as if someone else is telling it. It follows a process of objective analysis, taking *you* out of the equation to be replaced by *someone*, by (Mr or Ms) x, and then, once you have crafted the story or the scenario, imaginatively projecting yourself back into that world. Thus you can consider what it would be like for you to live in the circumstances resulting from a decision made in one direction or the other five or ten years earlier.

Yet another benefit of getting an outside view, though, is that thinking through your future on your own can get quite knotty. You can find yourself falling deeper into the pattern of trying to second-guess how your future self might respond to something which hasn't happened yet, and then trying to trace it back to where you are now to what you could or should do, and then back again. You end up swimming amongst lots of confusing sentences like 'in the future, I would x because I would have done y' and before you know it, you're having a weird kind of imaginary conversation across time with your future self about how you would have responded to stuff you haven't yet done. You follow? Messy. If it starts to feel like you are playing a kind of twisted game theory with your future self, you should stop immediately and go and have a cup of tea and ideally a bit of outside help.

Getting an outside view

'You know, somebody actually complimented me on my driving today. They left a little note on the windscreen, it said "Parking Fine".'
– Tommy Cooper

However great your intentions, however much you prime yourself to see yourself from the outside in, nothing can match getting a genuine outside view on your issues. The Internet now offers limitless possibilities to tell your story and have someone you don't know tell you whether you are right or wrong, and what you should do about it. While the anonymity can liberate you from concerns about self-exposure, it also potentially frees your judge from concerns about hurting your feelings. If you're going to ask, there are no lack of people willing to tell you whether you are indeed *hot, or not.*

So tell us about your mother...

The Internet allows fabulous and almost limitless access to relatively objective opinion, although you do have to be aware of the biases of others. For some people, the Internet now stretches out as a never-ending psychiatrist's couch, with a long tail of self-appointed experts, baggage-laden perhaps, but ready with their diagnoses. Of course there are some parts of the World Wild Web where trolls lurk and the sensitive may be traumatised when their problem laid out earnestly attracts irrelevant bile and obscenity. However, I think what is far more noteworthy and interesting is the dynamic behind sites like www.askmetafilter.com, where members of the metafilter community clearly spend time and care crafting thoughtful and sensitive responses to the problems of people they do not know – surely some fodder there to progress current theories on altruism and game theory. However, the value of their objectivity must be balanced against the fact that as strangers they cannot be expert in you – your history, your sensitivities and so on.

The bare bones

One benefit of turning to the crowd for answers is that it forces you to boil your dilemma down to the key salient points. A third party will only take so much detail. A similar dynamic applies to doing scenario planning on your dilemmas, forcing you to identify what is germane to the decision, and what are separate issues and anxieties with which you are conflating it. This can be highly beneficial. It is another example of how more corporate-style behaviour, the need to identify the essence of an argument when you present it, avoiding extraneous tangents, can be useful when dealing with some aspects of your personal life. The more distant someone is from you, the better able they are to be objective. On the other hand, the closer they are to you, the more expert they can be in *you* – who you are, what makes you tick, your likes and dislikes, what might make you happy.

Binoculars or microscope?

'Before you criticise someone, you should walk a mile in their shoes. That way when you criticise them, you are a mile away from them and you have their shoes.'
– Jack Handey

If you can, it is great to have somebody help you in your quest to be objective. The difficulty is, how close is *too* close? At what point does his or her knowledge of, and care about, you stray into what might be seen as too much certainty around what you need and what would be 'good for you'? The person who knows you really well may be burdened with too much knowledge about you and may lack the right perspective. Conversely, the person who doesn't know you at all may be capable of analysis which is too cold or 'impersonal', and irrelevant or disconnected to who you are. Furthermore, at either end of the scale they will have their own emotional baggage filtering their worldview. Is it better that you know their history and how they see the world, so you can then apply your own filters to what you hear from them?

There is an inverse relationship between the amount you know and trust someone and the expertise they have about you and their likely ability to be objective about you and your situation.

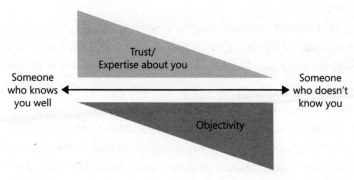

Figure 3

Better the devil you know – or turning to your friends

> *'Friends are helpful not only because they will listen to us,*
> *but because they will laugh at us; Through them we learn*
> *a little objectivity, a little modesty, a little courtesy; We learn*
> *the rules of life and become better players of the game.'*
> – Will Durant

Somewhere on the line between someone to whom you are close, whom you trust and who knows you really well, and someone who doesn't know you at all is the optimum point of trust and expertise about you and objectivity.

You are unlikely to have the perfect person to go to for any or all of your dilemmas. However, having a couple of advisers – or even a panel! – to go to when you want to get a bit of perspective is really helpful. Think carefully about who you go to for what. What kind of views and advice, if any, do you get from people you speak to? Who do you turn to for a sympathetic ear and who for a ruthless judgement? The person who is great at listening to you vent is unlikely to be the one who can tell you to just stop texting him, and the person who can give you the best work advice may well be someone else yet again. Your family may have the best insight into how a very personal question would affect you, but are likely to bring along their own extreme biases.

In business, 'Delphic research' is an accepted method of finding something out, and it involves going to a group of experts on a particular subject where you know you have a gap. (The term 'Delphic' originally derived from the prophesies of the priestess at the ancient Greek oracle at Delphi.) For futures studies, the Delphi method is a very particular way of getting a group of experts to interact and assess the probability, significance and implications of elements relating to a particular problem. Delphic research can be a thorough and considered way to analyse and gather data, or, I'm afraid, a euphemism for asking a few random people because there is not enough budget for proper research. Regardless of abuse of the term, the idea of going outside for views and expertise is a useful tactic and makes fundamental sense whatever your problem.

Mother knows best

I once designed a global study aiming to get a sense of emerging attitudes and behaviours in a world described by the sociologist Ulrich Beck as the 'Risk Society', a world where trust in traditional institutions such as government departments and the press had declined to the point where people no longer felt they could go to them for direction or advice on key life decisions such as finance, health and education. We had a sense that people were forging new trust networks, but we wanted to be able to quantify this. What emerged was a fascinating pattern of where consumers were seeking (and finding) their optimum point on the personal trust/ objectivity line.

For example, we asked people who they would go to to get advice about taking out a loan. The first person they would turn to was their partner if they had one, followed by their mother, then a friend, only then their father, and trailing behind was any kind of independent financial adviser. Not great news for the financial industry but we found ourselves suggesting a whole new group marketing model for business. (The study took place in the early 2000s – could we take credit for foreseeing the social media revolution?)

Look around

Most of us are surrounded by an array of potential resource to help us plan our futures better. We mine these informally, automatically, without thought when we go to our friends for support and gossip and affirmation. There's no reason why we can't also do this in a more planned, systematic way from time to time.

7

Combining Complexity (Modelling Your Future)

'Our conscious motivations, ideas, and beliefs are a blend of false information, biases, irrational passions, rationalizations, prejudices, in which morsels of truth swim around and give the reassurance albeit false, that the whole mixture is real and true. The thinking processes attempt to organize this whole cesspool of illusions according to the laws of plausibility. This level of consciousness is supposed to reflect reality; it is the map we use for organising our life.'
– Erich Fromm[63]

Here, the psychologist Eric Fromm taps into something very important. He acknowledges that the way we act and the decisions we make do not spring from the spur of the moment, but are shaped by a whole range of pre-existing factors, feelings and impulses. Humans are programmed in such a way which makes absolute objectivity near impossible. To add another level of complexity, as well as these internal drivers, our choices are also shaped by macro factors and external forces. In a world so complex, how can we imagine the system in which we live? How can we combine factors, assess probabilities, deal with risk on a personal scale without, well, getting too personal?

63   Fromm, Erich. *To Have or to Be? The Nature of the Psyche.* Rev. ed. London: Continuum, 2005.

This chapter is about getting people to improve how they deal with the different things that drive them and their future, pointing out some of the irrational baggage so it can be parked and we can move forward more smartly. How can you understand how your life and your world is affected by broader factors, how different variables interconnect? What narratives do we tell? How do we calculate risk and probability? How should we? It is about looking at things to a sufficient level of complexity – not so complex to be paralyzed by chaos but sufficiently so that there is some point, some weight to the logic.

Just toast

'Brains are for anticipating the future so that timely steps can be taken in better directions'.
– Daniel Dennett, *Freedom Evolves*[64]

It is a human imperative to look for a reason for things, a narrative, however flawed. We impose a structure of causality, even where none exists. I *could* say that the reason I got sacked from the job was because of burnt toast: I was sacked because after my warning about lateness I was late on the day of the visit from Head Office because I missed the bus because I couldn't find the keys in the dark because the fuse blew because I stuck a knife down the toaster because I burnt the toast. So I was toast because of the toast. But maybe it was the bus timetable, or the landlord's fault because of the electrics, or maybe my fault for being late to work once too often.

Where people place the cause of various personal outcomes, especially negative ones, provides an interesting insight into how

---

64   Dennett, Daniel. *Freedom Evolves*. New ed. London: Penguin, 2004.

they see the world and their own psychological make-up. This goes back to the locus of control idea (see Chapter 5). Extreme views on the causality of either positive or negative outcomes, either blaming everything on other people or outside forces, or seeing yourself as the cause of all, would suggest some delusional imbalance (paranoia or 'superpower' syndrome).

Sometimes we can try our best or do our worst but actually it doesn't make any difference to the outcome. I might be much more likely to lose my job due to company shrinkage and general redundancy than being fired for a misdemeanour. Difficult times may lead to a zero tolerance policy towards infractions which a year earlier would have provoked nothing more than silent disapproval. Some people are capable of refreshing honesty about their own agency, even where it comes to their own achievements. This was elegantly encapsulated by John Paul Getty, the multimillionaire oil baron, when asked about the secret of his success: 'Rise early, work hard, strike oil'! Sometimes things do just come down to chance.

However, chance is, alas, unreliable, far more unreliable than we like to admit: 'Chance is commonly viewed as a self-correcting process in which a deviation in one direction induces a deviation in the opposite direction to restore the equilibrium.' [65]

This is the 'gambler's fallacy', the belief that a coin which has flipped a successive row of ten heads is more likely to then show tails. This kind of fallacy pervades the way we speak (and think), encapsulated for example in the idea that someone's luck has run out, or conversely that a bad run will be followed by a lucky break. Luck – you just can't count on it.

---

65   Tversky, A. and D. Kahneman. 'Judgement Under Certainty: Heuristics and Biases', *Science*, 185 (4157), 1974.

Does it fit the story?

It turns out that the belief that lemmings deliberately jump off cliffs into the sea to commit mass suicide is a myth. Those that drown are the unfortunate few who never make it to the other side of an overly challenging body of water during migration. However, the makers of the 1958 Disney Film *White Wilderness* were having none of that. For the film, they flew in a bunch of unfortunate non-native lemmings to Alberta in Canada. There they repeatedly filmed the same handful of lemmings to make them look like a big mass of lemmings migrating, followed by the expected suicidal leaps into oblivion. However, this was not the instinctive lemming euthanasia programme of legend, tortured rodents voluntarily saying goodbye to this cruel world. Rather it was later revealed that the lemmings had no choice: 'just off camera there was a turntable, flinging the lemmings out and over the cliff.'[66]

Unlucky for the lemmings, but lucky for the makers of the film who won an Academy Award for Best Documentary Feature. Perhaps, at least for the lemmings, the moral of this story is 'fame costs'. But it's amazing how much people are willing to distort or ignore to be able to forge a good story, or to keep one going. If we cannot see a pattern, then it looks like chaos and chaos is uncomfortable. (Though not as uncomfortable as being flung off a turntable into the sea.) We need to make sense of the world around us, and will tend to fit what we see into our ideas rather than the other way round.

---

66   *Cruel Camera*, Canadian Broadcasting Corporation, 1982.

Biased? I knew it

'No man is born perpendicular'

– E.B. White

No one facing any decision, or at least self-aware enough to *realise* that they are facing a decision, comes at it truly as a *tabula rasa*, a blank slate. We need to make sense of the world around us, and will tend to fit what we see into our ideas rather than the other way round. We try to fit things into our existing model of understanding, seek earlier experiences and perceptions which may have bearing. Confirmation bias is 'an error of inductive inference toward confirmation of the hypothesis under study'[67], i.e. the tendency we all have to highlight things which confirm how we already think, giving more weight to data which support our existing view. More than this, we may actively seek out only those things which are consistent with our existing view. It is most obvious, at least to others, around issues that are emotionally charged or have a conspiratorial edge: gun control, homeopathy, 'feral' youth, that problem with your cousin.

There is a great website, www.literallyunbelievable.org. It's a collection of people's comments on Facebook who seem to have believed satirical stories from *The Onion* to be true. These go from appeals to pray and talk to your congressman for the sake of 'The Brain Dead Teen, Only Capable of Rolling Eyes and Texting, To Be Euthanised', to excitement that 'Intelligent Condescending Life Discovered in Distant Galaxy', to outrage at 'the closedmindedness' apparent from 'Transgendered Sea Anemone Denounced as "Abomination" by Clergy'. It seems that people

---

67   http://www.sciencedaily.com/articles/c/confirmation_bias.htm

have an incredible willingness (and some elasticity) to believe that which falls into line with existing views.

Why do we do it? Well it's simpler not to be challenged by what we see, to rely on existing mental models: the 'most likely reason for the excessive influence of confirmatory information is that it is easier to deal with cognitively' [68]. Confirmation bias is just one of a raft of 'intuitive heurestics', of selective thinking, which have received a lot of attention and analysis of late: affect bias, anchoring, inattentional blindness – the list goes on. Many great academics have written articulately and persuasively on how these mental tics distort our thinking. If you haven't already, just Google 'behavioural economics' or 'cognitive bias' and your world will open up.

...what do you mean? You're the one with the dirty pictures!

If you didn't recognise it, the above is the punchline to a joke about the Rorschach inkblot test. A man goes to the doctor having been accused of being able to think about nothing other than sex, and interprets a different sexual scene in all of the abstract inkblot pictures he is shown. The punchline is how he responds to the diagnosis that he is indeed sex-obsessed. The patient here is in denial, unable to see the evidence which is put in front of him, or unable to unsee it, as it were. As well as just being interesting because it shows us how our mental processes are pulled by hidden strings, an understanding of our biases may help us to counter their negative effects to some extent. Biases come out of the closet into the light of day.

---

68   Gilovich, Thomas. *How We Know What Isn't So: The Fallibility of Human Reason in Everyday Life*. New York: The Free Press, 1993.

Looking good

Biases are not all bad. Or at least an optimistic outlook might be a good kind of bias. Martin Seligman is Director of the Positive Psychology Centre at the University of Pennsylvania and a founder of positive psychology, 'a branch of psychology which focuses on the empirical study of such things as positive emotions, strengths-based character, and healthy institutions.' He would argue that the optimistic person is far more resilient than the pessimistic one because they have a particular response to setbacks and victories. Faced with a setback, the optimist believes 'it is temporary, I can change it, and it's just this one situation'[69].

However, exaggerated optimism brings its own dangers as optimism can lead to an appetite for excessive risk. This appetite for excessive risk stems from overconfidence in one's own decisions and the likely outcome of events. In *Thinking, Fast and Slow*[70], Daniel Kahneman records several painful examples, from inventors who have persisted despite being told by an objective assessment that their project had no hope of commercialisation, to new motel owners who have sunk their life-savings into their motel project even though the six previous owners had failed. He focuses on the danger of how in certain professions there is a requirement that a high degree of certainty be displayed, e.g. ICU doctors where expert overconfidence is encouraged by clients. 'An unbiased appreciation of uncertainty is a cornerstone of rationality – but it is not what people and organizations want. Extreme uncertainty is paralyzing under dangerous circumstances, and the admission that one is merely guessing is especially unacceptable when the stakes are high. Acting on pretended knowledge is often the preferred solution.'[71]

69   Dr Seligman's Definition of Optimism, YouTube.
70   Kahneman, Daniel. *Thinking, Fast and Slow*. London: Allen Lane, 2011.
71   Ibid.

In our interview, he asserted how hard it is to get people to change their behaviour, and that I was very optimistic in writing this book. There was no mention of exaggerated optimism, however, so maybe it *will* all turn out fine.

Dealing with data

We are allegedly living in the era of data. Not just data, but *big data*. New words are being coined to describe the unimaginable quantities of data being amassed, from megabytes to gigabytes to terabytes to petabytes, exabytes, zettabytes and yottabytes. Everywhere we go, everything we do, we leave a trail of bits grouped into bytes, of choices made, of options ignored. Sophisticated algorithms use this data to tailor our search results, decide our creditworthiness, plan our route and surround us with tempting deals. Yet we still have free will, for now, even if we are only getting to exercise it within our *Filter Bubble*. We are daily called on to make risk assessments, guess at probabilities and determine causality. We judge the trajectory of an oncoming car, assess the risk of a potentially subversive comment, gauge the worth of an insurance premium, or try to work out why the washing machine is making that noise.

Given how frequently we are called upon to make these kind of judgements in our personal lives, it is remarkable how poorly we tend to deal with risk, logic and probability. Despite the sophisticated demands the world places on us, and despite (or it sometimes seems it could be because of) expectations of logical thinking at work, we often fall very short of smart calculations when it comes to our personal lives.

Quantified self improvement

This issue is only going to get more urgent and obvious as the data mountain builds, and consumers increasingly have the opportunity to record and take control of their own data and use it to anticipate their own behaviour, in the way that corporations use, for example, retail spending data, to lure us into buying more. The philosophy behind this book is that people can and should seek as far as possible to rationally manage and improve their futures. The way is open.

We could change and improve our own lives by learning how to analyse this new personal data. We too should be able to spot patterns to make better decisions, but now in our own interests, joining the dots to make better sense of our own lives. Unlike the government or commercial organisations which collect data within limited silos, we will increasingly have access to data from many different areas of our life – not just spending, but health, mood, relationships. There is a huge opportunity, and even a responsibility, to be smart about the data, and not just leave it all to the organisations who can be bothered to collect it, or to the devices which can blindly lead us to drive off cliffs.

With the rise of smartphones, we now all have the potential to track data about ourselves, to join what has been called the 'Quantified Self' movement. If this is to become the 'Quantified Self-Improvement' movement, then we will also need to be able to analyse the data in smart ways, and not just be satisfied by whatever pre-fabricated template comes with the app.

Your number's up

Sometimes we knowingly mislead ourselves about our possible futures. Who has not been guilty of wiling away hours thinking about what would happen if we won the Lottery, if we got a promotion or were offered a job abroad? In these cases, if somebody were to confront us we would probably admit that we are not making a sensible calculation, but unchallenged we carry on. Perhaps the best term here is 'half-knowing', a kind of sub-conscious awareness that hums quietly but is quickly quieted when acknowledged, often with irony. That we buy Lottery tickets at all, for example, which I once heard described as 'a tax on the mathematically challenged'. We are fine as long as we expect and can deal with the disappointment all but guaranteed by the poor odds and are not excessively fixated on the potential reward.

Alas, there are plenty of examples where people have let miscalculations get the better of them, blowing events and possible consequences far beyond the bounds of proportion. Timothy O'Brien, for example, who shot himself after believing he had missed out on a £1m win because his lottery ticket had expired. In fact, the ticket would have yielded him only £27[72]. 'It could be you', as the UK National Lottery slogan promises. It could be, but I'm afraid it's most unlikely. As Michael Argyle, a psychologist, suggested, 'People should play the lottery by all means, but they should try not to win. Given the odds, this advice is fairly easy to follow.'[73]

The Darwin Awards confers posthumous congratulations on 'those who make the world a safer place for all by not reproducing', victims of their own unbelievable miscalculations. But for most of us, poor calculations don't have such extreme results. Rather, they just mean we navigate the world a little less smartly, use our resources a little less efficiently, spend more money than we need to, waste more time than necessary, that results are *sub-optimal*.

---

72 As reported in *The Independent,* http://www.independent.co.uk/news/it-was-them-10-lottery-winners-and-losers-1581838.html
73 Michael Argyle, Oxford Brooks University. Quoted in *The Guardian,* 17 July 1999.

Personal wildcards and risk factors

As we saw in Chapter 3, corporate futures planning does not just cover likely events. It should also take account as far as possible of wildcards, low-probability high-impact events, even if these wildcards are ultimately sidelined from any resulting models. As individuals, we also face wildcards. On the positive side, winning the Lottery or finding out you do have the X Factor are very low probability events (sorry) which would have an enormous impact on your life. Some of society's current malaise could be put down to the poor calculations made by those who have miscalculated the probability that they will for example, be recognised by the judges as the ones who have *Got Talent*. On the other hand, one could argue that where all other options are unattractive, it is unsurprising that people miscalculate the odds and pin all their hopes on unlikely but fantastic outcomes, in the real sense of the word. It is a desperate, hopeful miscalculation.

On the negative side, personal wildcards would include being struck by a rare disease, a car crash, the untimely loss of a loved one (I'm not sure what the timely death of a loved one would mean, by the way). These are all low-probability events with devastating outcomes. How *should* we factor these in? How large *should* these events loom in our world view and planning? Surely if we were to let our lives become dominated by these possibilities, we would be paralysed with fear. Yet we are surprisingly unwilling to take sensible action. In the United Kingdom, more people insure their mobile phones than their income in case they become ill.[74]

How do we calculate risk? According to Professor Paul Slovic, one of the world's leading academics on the psychology of risk, there is no such thing as objective risk. Risk 'does not exist "out

---

there", independent of our minds and cultures, waiting to be measured. Instead, *risk* is seen as a concept that human beings have invented to help them understand and cope with the dangers and uncertainties of life'[75]. How we perceive risk matters, because it determines how we act.

Professor Slovic's work on risk includes a 'dread/knowledge spectrum'. Simply put, we tend to overestimate the odds and become excessively anxious over risks which are unobservable and which we cannot control. Thus people may be far more concerned about radioactive or chemical contamination from a factory, for example (cannot see it, results of contamination not immediately apparent, relatively uncontrollable), than the far more likely risk of being hurt in a traffic accident. Parents tend to feel far more anxiety about the possibility of someone snatching their child (invisible, uncontrollable enemy) than the far greater risk of drowning.

The behavioural economics canon has provided us with a comprehensive list of all the ways we bias the information we receive, distorting and misjudging the world around us. The UK government, amongst others, has taken on board some of the messages and experts in the many subtle ways our brains and our perception subvert rational decision-making in the hope that this knowledge can help us push behaviour in a more positive direction and *Nudge* us towards a better future.

The big picture

In general in large organisations it is only those at the top who have an overview of how it all works and can see the bigger picture. Lower down in the hierarchy such knowledge is not necessarily accessible,

---

75 *Perception of Risk Posed by Extreme Events*, Paul Slovic, Elke U. Weber, paper prepared for the conference 'Risk Management strategies in an Uncertain World', New York, April 12–13 2002.

and what's more, does not always help with the day job. People lower down the chain of command may not need to know how all the pieces of the machine operate and what their functions are. However, thinking about the future of the organisation as a whole is an incredibly powerful way to get people within different departments and at different levels to be allowed an awareness of what the whole organisation is doing. When it comes to our own lives we are the only ones who could really get the big picture. It's worth a try.

Systems thinking and causality

'Every decision you make affects every facet of every other
[...] thing. It's too much to deal with almost.
And in the end you're completely alone with it all.'
– Tony Soprano

How can we conceive of the world and where we sit in it? How should we understand the factors which combine to shift our positions, and how we can, in turn, move them, if at all? It is hard enough with the past, let alone the future. Even if history is written by the victors, they rarely agree on why things have turned out as they did. Some will insist we are where we are due to the actions and interventions of individuals. Others tell a compelling tale of conclusions reached through cod, or nutmeg, or guns, germs and steel, shipping containers or climate[76].

---

76 See: Kurlansky, Mark. *Cod: A Biography of the Fish Which Changed the World*. London: Vintage, 1999. Milton, Giles. *Nathaniel's Nutmeg: How One Man's Courage Changed the Course of History*. London: Sceptre, 2000. Diamond, Jared. *Guns, Germs and Steel: A Short History of Everybody for the last 13,000 years*. London: Vintage, 1998. Levinson, Marc: *The Box: How the Shipping Container Made the World Smaller and the World Economy Bigger*. Princeton, New Jersey: Princeton University Press, 2008. Fagan, Brian: *The Long Summer: How Climate Changed Civilisation*. London: Granta, 2004.

A living system

'We demand rigidly defined areas of doubt and uncertainty!'
— Douglas Adams, *The Hitchhiker's Guide to the Galaxy*

It may be surprising to learn that there is no perfect way to understand and model complex systems in business and life. Even the most scientific-looking model built by the geekiest mathematical genius will have had some element of art in it, at least in so far that they must have selected which variables to include and which to leave out. Regression analysis is the rather fearful name given to the technique in forecasting which attempts to understand and predict how different variables interact, to create models which can suggest which thing causes another. But certainty that we are looking at causation rather than correlation is usually a question of degree, not of absolutes.

It's an important thing to bear in mind when we are trying to understand the complexity of our own lives, to work out what caused what, to understand why he got that job, why I didn't get the promotion, what lead her to emigrate, what I need to do to get the prize.

The process for making a decision outlined in Chapter 8 requires some sense of your life as a system, in so far as it assumes that different factors are interdependent, having an impact on each other. The framework for thinking about a particular system is most often highlighted by unintended consequences, revealing the gaps in the system theory. Sometimes positive (such as when drugs designed to cure one thing also turn out to alleviate something else, as with aspirin), the law of unintended consequences is quoted most often when it leads to a negative outcome, when something unanticipated puts a spanner in the mental works. This becomes Murphy's Law (anything that can go wrong, will go wrong), otherwise known as Sod's Law when it includes a bit of irony, which generates Jenning's Corollary (the chance of the bread falling with the buttered side down is directly proportional to the cost of the carpet) and closely related to Finagle's Law (inanimate objects are out to get us).

I think the point is not to try to recreate a perfect systems model for how our life operates (we would end up with something completely unwieldy, like the accurate but useless map built on the scale of one-to-one in a Borges story, *On Exactitude in Science*). Rather we need to get to something which makes enough sense for us to be able to test out different scenarios. Enough sensible connections and causality for us to be able to persuade a smart friend, say, that we have thought things through.

Goldilocks complexity

It is just as possible to invite too much complexity, to look in too much detail, as to oversimplify. Many people follow house price movements monthly, when a house purchase may come once in decades, and even when there may be no prospect of selling or buying or even leveraging their property. Others track currency movements with a frequency which would only be useful and meaningful to Forex traders, but relatively meaningless to those who take a biannual foreign holiday.

While there are those people who seem happy to remain ignorant of world events, there are also those who seem to feel that everything is on a need to know basis. Just because we can now have 24-hour rolling news, does not mean it deserves our attention non-stop. It is the job of the newsmakers and distributors to fill the channel, not ours to drink it all in.

Not too much and not too little – most people can take a little bit more. Or, as Einstein put it, 'everything should be made as simple as possible, but no simpler'.

8

Futurescaping: The Personal Version of Scenario Planning

---

*'I think myself that the best sort of futurist story should be one
that sets out to give you the illusion of reality.
It ought to produce the effect of a historical novel,
the other way round. It ought to read like fact.'*

– H.G. Wells[77]

So we've seen how companies need to look beyond the immediate question to manage risk and create strategy. Now it's time to take that logic out of the workplace and apply it to the big choices in our lives. This is a method to help you factor in the broader implications of a key decision you may face. You do this by looking at the decision and robustly imagining different futures based on the ways you could take that decision, exploring the key drivers which are related to it, and working through how they would impact your life if you decided one way or the other.

The stories of these different futures, the scenarios, will help you make that key decision. However, the usefulness of the exercise is not just in the final scenarios, but also in the way that framing and analysing a decision in this way brings new clarity of thought and encourages other relevant issues to surface. As we have seen in

---

77   Parrinder, Patrick, and Robert M. Philmus. *H.G. Wells's Literary Criticism*. Brighton: Harvester Press, 1980.

Chapter 3, any kind of planning which allows for uncertainty is going to be more useful and effective than one which doesn't.

How traditional scenario planning works

Scenario planning is slowly becoming a staple of the corporate toolbox. Formal scenarios were first used after the Second World War as a method for war game analysis[78]. The technique of scenario planning really developed in the United States in the 1950s and 1960s, when the Cold War stimulated policy-makers to seek new ways of looking at the world. There is some controversy as to who can take the most credit for inventing the scenario-planning techniques which are used today. Most agree, however, that the American Herman Kahn played a central role. He was working for the Rand Corporation at the time, a non-profit organisation initially designed to 'connect military planning with research and development decisions'[79] following 1945. Kahn really become famous (or notorious) in 1960 when he published *On Thermonuclear War*[80], forcing a dreaded but largely unarticulated prospect out into the public domain.

Herman Kahn himself was a highly controversial figure. He advocated a deliberately unsettling and often subversive way of presenting the possible, shocking many of his contemporaries, for example, with what some took as an excessively lighthearted approach to presenting the horrors of nuclear war. But Kahn believed it was the best way to get people to open their minds. 'Awe is fine for those who come to worship or admire, but for those who come to analyze, to tamper, to change, to criticize...sometimes

---

78   Van der Heijden, Kees. *The Art of Strategic Conversation*. Hoboken, New Jersey: Wiley, 1996.
79   www.rand.org
80   Kahn, Herman. *On Thermonuclear War*. Princeton, New Jersey: Princeton University Press, 1960.

a colorful approach is preferred.' [81] It is Kahn's particular brand of humour and the grotesque which Stanley Kubrick injected into the film *Dr Strangelove*, turning it from the serious film about nuclear war which Kubrick had originally intended to a black comedy, even though many critics of the time saw it as simply a sick joke designed to undermine the defence establishment.

Kahn embraced the idea of 'thinking the unthinkable' as a way to keep strategic vision fresh, and this spirit was taken on elsewhere. The technique of scenario planning was further developed by the fabulously named Pierre Wack at Shell for business planning in the 1970s and 1980s, and Shell is now the business most closely associated with the technique. Many of those who have ensured scenario planning's place as a central plank of the futures and planning canon were originally exposed to it while working for Shell.

At its most elevated, scenario planning is a technique to free the imagination. According to Art Kleiner, another one of the leading lights of the technique, Pierre Wack used to compare scenario planning to zen archery, as 'a way to hone your senses until you can see the world as it really is'[82]. Kleiner believed that it enables us 'to learn to visualise the possible worlds in which the unimaginable, the unthinkable and the ungodly, and the unpredictable actually come to pass'[83]. Scenario planning can change the world. The Mont Fleur scenarios, for example, carried out in South Africa 1991–92, are credited with playing an important role in ending apartheid and forging a path for democracy.

The technique appeals to those with a scientific bent, impressed by how it marshals messy reality into clean lines and logical paths.

---

81 Ghamari-Tabrizi, Sharon. *The Worlds of Herman Kahn*, Cambridge, Massachusetts: Harvard University Press, 2005.
82 Quoted in www.wholeearth.com.
83 Ibid.

The mathematical element can be turned up, for example by constructing dependency matrices to identify dependency between different drivers (see point 3 on p. 121), using complex mathematical models to assess probability (and thus identify the most uncertain driver), or assigning and then aggregating scores to select the most important one. Those of a less mathematical bent can engage most immediately with the content of the drivers and the myriad different ways the scenarios may turn out, and of course a good story appeals to everyone.

The power of stories

Stories can be powerful things. This is just as true in a business context as elsewhere. A number of academic studies have confirmed and amplified the findings of one first carried out in 1982 in which four methods were tested to persuade a group of MBA students of a hypothesis (that a Californian winery had improved its products on the basis that they were using French wine techniques for making Chablis), a story, statistical data, statistical data and a story, and a policy statement. The story proved the most persuasive[84]. Stories can find a place to engage people in the most hard-headed of businesses. They allow the future to be explored without risk. This is not to say that any old story will do, however: they have to be meaningful to the audience, engaging with their imagination but also with sufficient detail to bring it to life. As Mike Roberts, the ex-President of McDonald's and a veteran of the technique put it: 'I

---

84   Martin, J. and Powers, M. 'Organizational Stories: More Vivid and Persuasive than Quantitative Data'. In *Psychological Foundations of Organizational Behavior*. Longman Higher Education (1983). See also Brown, M. H. (1990). 'Defining stories in organizations: Characteristics and functions'. In J. Anderson (Ed.), *Communication Yearbook* 13 (pp. 162-190). Thousand Oaks, California: Sage Publications. Also: Denning, S. (2000). *The Springboard: How Storytelling Ignites Action in Knowledge-Era Organizations*. Oxford: Butterworth-Heinemann, 2000.

would, with support, paint that future picture as vividly and succinctly and detailed as I could, and I would be expressing the tumultuous scenario of the open sea at the same time.[85]

The scenario process

As a process, the bare bones of what has now become classic scenario planning run as follows:

1. First, identify your question. This can be more difficult than it sounds. The question has to be sufficiently broad to require and encourage the imagination, but sufficiently grounded for the answer to be meaningful and useful for whoever is asking it. How can we build democratic institutions in South Africa? What is the future for the music industry? What will be the role of TV in advertising? What will the food store of the future look like?

2. Next, identify the different drivers which will have an impact on that question over the next ten years (or however far ahead you are looking). So if we take the last question about the food store of the future as an example, that could include issues around food supply, retail margins and rents, economic outlook and consumer spending, environmental, ethical and provenance factors, CSR concerns, consumer health issues, the roles and responsibilities of retail brands towards health and consumption, the strength of retail vs manufacturing brands, new developments in logistics, social media evolution, consumer technology adoption, augmented reality, price attitudes, consumer data and privacy attitudes, online-offline relationship, changing attitudes to customer service, retail staffing, regulatory change etc. In turn, it can provide the basis for strategy for everything from what and how to sell and how to communicate

85   In conversation with the author.

with the customer to planograms – store maps which show how the merchandise is laid out.

3. Usually via a series of workshops, the team analyses each driver in turn. They check to see if all of them seem valid and if any have been missed. Then they go on to identify the two which they feel are most important, which would have the biggest impact on the question, and which are also most uncertain, because if something is certain then it will happen regardless of which scenario emerges. This is when the Post-it® Notes usually come out, and the walls get covered with evolving clusters as participants try to make sense of a complex array of interconnecting drivers.

4. Once they have agreed on the two which are both the most important and the most uncertain, they then have the parameters of an x-axis and a y-axis. Typically, these two drivers are expressed as continua, for example economic boom vs recession, or consumers open to brands vs consumers less open to brands, rather than either/or binary labels. Ideally, the selection of drivers is subject to rigorous testing. Do they make sense? Does the logic hold up?

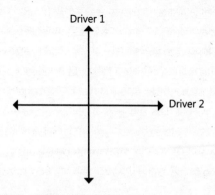

Figure 4: Diagram with driver 1 and 2

5. The two axes provide the parameters to define four different scenarios for how the future could pan out. These are then drawn up as richly as possible, but always trying to keep in mind the original question and how the scenarios are to be used ultimately. All the discussion and analysis from steps 1–3 will have highlighted the key issues which should be covered to make the scenarios meaningful and relevant.

One way to think about this is as writing the story, the plot, for how converging forces might intersect. The plot motif helps because for these scenarios to come to life they need to engage people with a compelling story about the future. Peter Schwartz, in *The Art of the Long View*, describes it as having a similar breadth of direction and texture as any 'story of a man meeting a woman. It's one of the oldest plots in the world. It can either be handled sentimentally, in a manner full of clichés (as in the movie *Love Story*), or in a wonderfully original and moving fashion (as in *A Man and Woman*). Either way, it's the same story – but what a difference! Scenarios, too, can be formulaic or moving, depending on how you think about the plots.'[86]

The most narrowly focused scenario project I ever ran was for a global FMCG company looking to improve their logistical modeling. We went through a scenario process about retail which was designed to arrive at upper and lower limits for the profit margins at particular stages within the supply chain. It was not *Love Story* but it seems to have moved the Logistical Planning department nonetheless.

6. Once the scenarios have been drawn up they are ready to feed into the development of strategy. What vulnerabilities and opportunities have been revealed? When the scenarios are rehearsed what

---

86   Schwartz, Peter. *The Art of the Long View*. Hoboken, New Jersey: Wiley, 1997.

strategy makes sense in response? Are there strategies to be pursued which make sense for more than one scenario? If so, should we consider pursuing them straight away? The organisation may also develop a series of early warning systems to be able to anticipate which scenarios seem to be developing.

7. Ideally, the scenario planning exercise is not an endpoint but part of an ongoing interest in understanding the future.

Let's get personal

This chapter sets out a way to take some of the essential elements of scenario planning to apply them to individuals. Simply taking the traditional scenario planning process as is and trying to use it as a personal level doesn't work; it requires some modification. Some scenario planning purists might find this upsetting. If so they should stop reading here and tear this chapter out and make it into origami.

As with traditional scenario planning, when it comes to planning for individuals, thinking widely and thoroughly is essential. The PEST (political, economic, social, technological) model for drivers can be a useful starting point to unearth and explore the areas which will be impacted by a decision in a particular sphere. Whether you have a decision to make about your career or your car, just going through and ticking off the different factors can be a good way to get you thinking about PEST in your life. While these 'macro' factors are not always the primary or prioritised factors, scenario planning works somewhat like a funnel. These inputs are crucial and help provide a more robust picture of a personal landscape for the scenario planner. They will form implicit assumptions in your scenarios, if not explicit ones.

PEST is usually assumed to refer to macro drivers affecting societies on a regional if not global scale. We could leave them at that level, but we can also modify them to a more intimate level so they make sense on a personal scale, and the model can be used to stimulate thinking when it comes to individual dilemmas.

For example, P –political, the most tricky one, we could take it to be P for power, career, or P for promotion.

E – Economic – incomings (usually salary) and outgoings (rent, mortgage, sustenance, money for needs, money for wants. Or E for entertainment and hobbies.

S – Social – community and relationship ties, social status, approval or censure.

T – Technological, or T for Travel, location.

We can add a D for Dependants, H for Health, E for Ethical or environmental...

It may be jarring to be so reductionist, but even though you are truly special, this is simply a way to categorise what influences your life so we can be sure we are thinking widely enough. It will also help us structure and 'frame' planning.

Which way now?

Have you ever gone to the supermarket as an anthropologist? It's worth having a go at a bit of people-watching. Some customers just grab and go but others spend ages agonising in the supermarket aisles, trying to make a decision about lunch or dinner: contemplating the cost, the preferences of their fellow diners perhaps, their food history, the ethics of their food choices, or seemingly just gazing at the patterns on the boxes. Hands hover over a packet, sometimes a shifty-eyed look to the side, an unhealthy choice being considered, perhaps. Something picked up, scrutinised, then put back. Precious time spent over a sandwich choice, and then a rush through life's big decisions, eyes closed. Can't be right.

Now, getting back to you. Imagine the decision you are facing, any big decision which you regard to be important to the future of your life. While people often appreciate that a decision is important to them, it is rare that the decision is given sufficient time and quality of thought. Often, most time and mental energy is focused on the emotional burden of being faced with that decision as it sits there, leaden, weighing us down. We are all susceptible to procrastinating about even the most momentous decisions, generally because they are so momentous. Logic and rationality, easily called upon when making small decisions, just seem to fall away.

So what do we do?

How can we redress the balance? What are the steps we can follow to help us reapportion the right amount of attention to what is more important? The first thing to do is to identify a big decision you are facing and work out why it is important. (This is the first departure from classic scenario planning, where the initial question is not an either/or dilemma, even if what comes out at the end is used to answer a binary question.)

As part of researching this book, a number of people were kind enough to let us test the process with them on a wide range of different life decisions. We've selected from this group those which can best illustrate the theory and process of futurescaping (anonymising them as much as they requested).

As a way to take you through the process, let's start with an example of Inès, whose decision and futurescaping was fairly straightforward. The later case studies will help demonstrate how the process would work with different questions and increasing levels of complexity (two people involved, more areas of life being impacted, more complex circumstances).

Inès was wrestling with the decision of whether or not to get a dog. The question of whether to buy a pet or not may seem trivial to some, but it is one which has surprisingly long-term implications. Believe it or not, pets, like children, careers, and investments, require future planning. According to VetUK, the average dog costs the owner £15,000 over the course of its life. To all of you who read 'pet-buying' and dismissed it as an unimportant life-choice, how would your life be altered if every day for the next 5–10 years you had to care for a dog? This animal would have to be factored into all of your daily decisions: should you take a promotion which will mean longer hours? Who will look after it if you want to take a mini-break or holiday? Perhaps you won't be able to afford gym membership if there's a big vet bill?

Inès's choice

Inès is a financial journalist in her late twenties. She had recently bought a small flat in an affluent area of Leeds where she lives alone and was deliberating whether to get a dog. Inès had wanted a dog for a long time. However, she had previously lived in rented accommodation and therefore pets were contractually not allowed. With her busy and unpredictable work commitments and a busy social life, she was trying to decide whether a dog is compatible with her lifestyle. While the majority of the time she keeps to typical office hours, there have been periods of time when her workload has been increased and consequently her lifestyle and work/life balance has altered. She loved the idea of having a dog, but had held back from any decision due to a vague unease that she might regret it.

We talked through her choice and the starting point was turning her decision into a question to herself: should I get a dog or not?

Dog or no dog? We discussed why this decision was important to her. Inès revealed that a dog would impact on key areas of her life and we established that while it could bring her a lot of companionship and pleasure it also brought complications.

Most of the big decisions that we face fall within a limited number of separate but interrelated life spheres, which make up modern life. In turn, a question in any of these spheres will impact a range of different areas. In the same way that successful futures planning for companies requires an openness to drivers which are beyond the internal issues of the company, successful future planning for individuals is also enhanced by an understanding of the potential far-reaching implications of a decision in one sphere. We will look at these spheres and their related impacts in a moment. In the meantime, back to Inès.

The first thing we had to do was identify the question, and work out which sphere of life the dilemma falls into. In Inès's case, the question was 'should I adopt a dog or not?' and the life sphere is clearly 'pet ownership'. We can draw a picture like this:

Should I adopt a
dog or not?
Pet Ownership

Figure 5

We discussed how in a lesser – but not dissimilar – way to a child, a pet brings responsibility, investment (of both time and money) and imposes limitations on travel, socialising and time away from the home. Inès listed all of the areas of her life which a pet would impact upon: working life, travel, social life, personal life, leisure time, finances and health. Once we had made this topline list of areas which might be affected by the pet decision, we went through and thought about each one in more detail – discussing the positive and, of course, negative implications of having a dog (or not).

For example, we took the impact on health. Inès is physically fit but often lacks the motivation to go running and felt that a dog would force her to regularly walk, jog or run. She felt that while she sometimes exercised with friends, a dog would be the stronger motivation to get out of the house. However, she was concerned that the time required to exercise the dog sufficiently might eat into the time she spent with friends.

This brought us to the impact a dog would have on her social life. A dog would not have a negative impact on her regular social activities such as dinner parties, gigs and clubbing. However, she revealed that this would limit her frequent weekend trips to friends in London or family in France. Also if she decided to stay out overnight, she would have to factor in feeding the dog, perhaps before work. A dog would also mean that more lengthy holidays would be more complicated and that she would have to find a reliable kennel in the nearby area, something which would be an added expense. Conversely she thought that perhaps a dog would make her more inclined to holiday in England or possibly she could drive to France for longer holidays.

There would also be a financial impact in terms of dog food and vet bills, but Inès had worked it out and felt her budget could stretch comfortably.

On the plus side, Inès would be more inclined to spend time at home knowing she would be guaranteed a warm welcome and companionship. Also she felt that friends may be more inclined to visit with the added novelty of a dog and it would be a good icebreaker when making new friends. She hoped she might develop a circle of dog-owning friends, thus expanding her social circle. She wasn't concerned about the inevitable side-effects of dog ownership – chewed-up dog toys and dog hair – and didn't think her friends would be either. She would also be more inclined to organise social activities at her home and perhaps cook more dinners herself rather than eating out all the time.

All of these concerns are taking into account the PEST (political, economic, social and technological) factors but at a more personal scale, personal PEST. Are there any really macro factors Inès should consider? For example, Inès decided that the job market and opportunities for financial journalists could potentially have a big impact on the feasibility of dog ownership. If she were offered a job at Bloomberg and asked to re-locate to New York, for example, she would have to secure additional vaccinations and other health precautions for her dog. This would require extra time and money, besides the fact that she would have to find new living accommodations in a new city that would allow pets. It additionally could mean a traumatic experience for her pet with travel and getting acclimated to a new city.

This diagram below shows the broad areas on which her decision will have an impact:

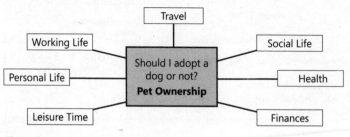

Figure 6

We repeated this discursive process to understand in more depth how each of the life areas Inès mentioned would be impacted by a dog. Why had she brought up that life area in the first place? Had anything changed, or was about to change? All of these would come in useful later in drawing up the scenarios.

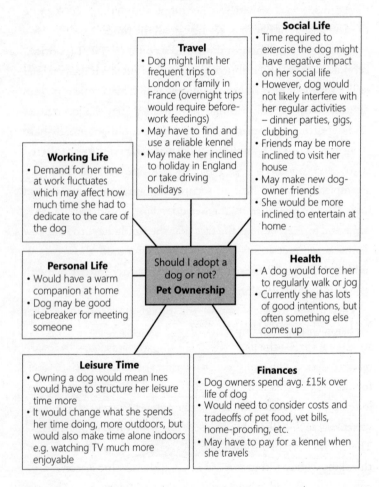

Social Life
- Time required to exercise the dog might have negative impact on her social life
- However, dog would not likely interfere with her regular activities – dinner parties, gigs, clubbing
- Friends may be more inclined to visit her house
- May make new dog-owner friends
- She would be more inclined to entertain at home

Travel
- Dog might limit her frequent trips to London or family in France (overnight trips would require before-work feedings)
- May have to find and use a reliable kennel
- May make her inclined to holiday in England or take driving holidays

Working Life
- Demand for her time at work fluctuates which may affect how much time she had to dedicate to the care of the dog

Personal Life
- Would have a warm companion at home
- Dog may be good icebreaker for meeting someone

Should I adopt a dog or not?
Pet Ownership

Health
- A dog would force her to regularly walk or jog
- Currently she has lots of good intentions, but often something else comes up

Leisure Time
- Owning a dog would mean Ines would have to structure her leisure time more
- It would change what she spends her time doing, more outdoors, but would also make time alone indoors e.g. watching TV much more enjoyable

Finances
- Dog owners spend avg. £15k over life of dog
- Would need to consider costs and tradeoffs of pet food, vet bills, home-proofing, etc.
- May have to pay for a kennel when she travels

Figure 7

The matrix

Once we had covered all these bases as comprehensively as possible, we were ready to begin to draw up what would become our 4-box scenario matrix.

The first step is to draw a horizontal line, the x-axis. This is the basic decision axis, with the binary options at either end. In Inès's case, on the left of the horizontal line we wrote **No Dog**, and the right we have **Dog**.

So here we have our x-axis:

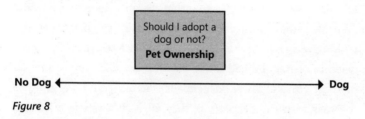

Figure 8

It should appear to you as a straight line and a straight choice which you are posing to yourself.

Getting to the 'superdriver'

We then reviewed the list of different impact areas. Now Inès was ready to decide which of the factors would be an appropriate label for the y-axis. This is a tricky part of the process, where we are looking for the factor which is to become the y-axis, the second variable, which will enable us to define four different scenarios. There is no right or wrong y-axis. In corporate scenario planning, this tends to be the step which takes the most time and concentration, and where disagreements tend to arise (before being resolved by a skilled facilitator). We did this by evaluating each of the drivers in detail to determine which were both independent of the decision she was making *and* uncertain.

To elaborate, it needed to be something which *could* vary regardless of whether Inès got a dog or not, rather than being something which was simply a function of, would be driven by, whether or not she got a dog. So we discounted health, as Inès felt that a positive health outcome would be essentially determined by whether she had a dog or not, and thus was a derivative of the x-axis. Travel also would be determined by whether she had the limitations imposed by a dog. Like her health, impact on travel would be determined by whether or not she had the commitments of a pet. (We are not suggesting that the only thing which would ever affect Inès's health was whether or not she had a pet, but within the context of this decision, as she had described the driver, whether or not she had a dog was the key issue impacting her physical fitness. These 'dependent' factors could be grouped together with the decision as they all have a relatively certain outcome which is dependent on her getting or not getting a dog.)

These dependent factors are the same in both the top and bottom quadrants. This factor tends to become blurred with the decision itself and therefore merge into the x-axis.

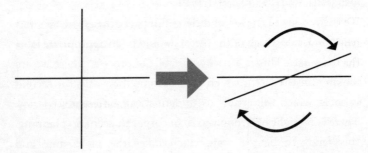

Figure 9

We worked through until we were left with 'career' and 'time availability'. We realised that her free time was determined by her job and how busy she was: whether or not there was a lot of work, and thus for the purposes of this decision they were essentially the same factor. Given she was assuming she would be staying in her current job and in her current flat, the amount of free time Inès has is the thing which would most affect her life with or without a pet. This, then, was the factor which Inès felt was the most important and also the most uncertain in so far as it could vary the most.

While free time was one of the areas which having a pet would impact (unlike the other factors which we had hitherto ruled out as y-axis candidates because they were entirely driven by the x-axis decision), it is something that could vary independently of pet ownership, and thus would provide a different outcome above and below the y-axis. Therefore, we felt available time was the most important factor for Inès, one which was free from dependency on the x-axis: whether or not Inès gets a dog, the volume of work, and therefore her free time, would vary. Furthermore, it would have a major impact on what her life would be like.

So now Inès had been able to identify the superdriver for her decision, and she had her y-axis to go with the x-axis.

The y-axis was labelled time with **Lots of time/normal workflow** at the top and **Little time/high demand for work** at the bottom.

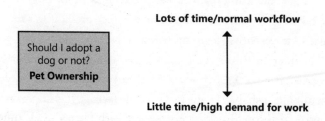

Figure 10

Then the x-axis:

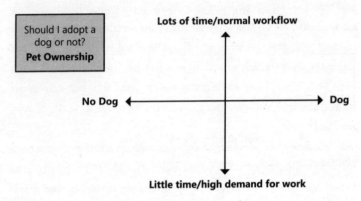

Figure 11

And now, with a bit of a fanfare, we have the parameters for Inès's scenarios for her dog question.

Inès was then ready to fill in the four different scenarios as fully as possible. In order to do this, she referred back to her detailed list of impact areas the dog issue relates to and wrote down the positive, or negative consequences of the factors. For example, in the top-right quarter where she has lots of time and a dog, her health has improved, she is enjoying emotional companionship from the dog and he is well-trained from time invested. She has a good work/life balance. Her social life is more centred around the flat but she has also expanded her social circle to include fellow dog owners. Her trips to London and France are however more limited – travel with a dog is more restrictive.

This diagram shows the in-depth pictures which were easily constructed once Inès thought in detail what her life would turn out like if shaped by the two variable factors. It is important to emphasise that these are not predictions. Rather, they are a topline portrait, a story of how Inès imagined her life in terms of how these life areas would be in five years' time if she had or had not bought a dog today, and based on how busy she was with work:

Should I adopt a
dog or not?
Pet Ownership

Lots of time/normal workflow

CAREER: Work is ok, stable
TRAVEL: Lots of time for travel to London and France
SOCIAL: Able to go out at a moment's notice and has time to see friends often
FINANCIAL: Able to use her spare cash on travel and herself
HEALTH: Makes an effort to exercise, but is hard to self motivate. Exercises with friends when possible
EMOTIONAL: Stable – perhaps missing companionship at her flat

CAREER: Normal workflow means lots of spare time
TRAVEL: Trips to London and France more limited
SOCIAL: More centered around her flat but has expanded social circle with new dog-owner friends
FINANCIAL: Could take on lodger for extra income
HEALTH: Increased exercise with dog means health is improved
EMOTIONAL: Enjoying companionship and emotional benefits of pet ownership

No Dog ◀—————————————————▶ **Dog**

CAREER: Increased work flow means she is getting ahead at work
TRAVEL: Trips to London and France more limited due to time but can afford to take spontaneous trips when schedule allows
SOCIAL: Able to go out at a moment's notice but sees less of friends due to work
FINANCIAL: Making good money and extra cash is spent on herself and travel
HEALTH: Exercise is sporadic
EMOTIONAL: Stable – spends little time at her flat due to work schedule

CAREER: Increased work flow means has to carefully manage work/life balance
TRAVEL: Trips to London and France more limited due to time and pet constraints
SOCIAL: More centered around her flat
FINANCIAL: Making good money, but some extra cash goes toward kennel
HEALTH: Increased exercise
EMOTIONAL: Enjoying companionship and emotional benefits of pet ownership when she can

Little time/high demand for work

Figure 12

What did Inès do?

Despite the unpredictability of Inès's work, she felt that after undertaking this exercise she had finally thought through the implications sufficiently and that the positive benefits of having a dog would outweigh the possible limitations it would impose. Before the process, she had seen herself choosing between a very free lifestyle and a very settled one, but through this exercise Inès realised that in having bought a flat she was already choosing a more settled, adult lifestyle which she really wanted, and that a dog was in keeping with this change in her life. If her work did become much more hectic, she felt that having a dog would ensure she didn't get too carried away, and would help her maintain a better work/life balance.

She also now felt she had a strategy for offsetting what had been some of the barriers to dog ownership (limits on travel), and a good sense of the kind of dog that she could best nurture within the constraints of her lifestyle. She decided to get a dog, and at time of writing is completing the paperwork to take home a dog from the rescue centre.

Should I adopt a dog or not? **Pet Ownership**

The outcome for Inès:
- Decided a dog would open up new opportunities
- Felt these would outweigh limitations of dog ownership
- Developed strategy for offsetting barriers to ownership
- Understood more clearly what kind of dog she could best nurture with her lifestyle
- Ultimately decided to adopt a dog from a rescue centre

Figure 13

Inès's view

'I found this exercise really helpful. Even though it did not make the decision *for* me, I felt that the right course of action was much clearer and more obvious by the time we had drawn up the four possible scenarios. It's often hard for me to see where my choices will lead, as I tend to get stressed about the immediate consequences and fail to see into the future. Instead, by looking forward towards the future it becomes much more obvious.

'All of my anxieties about getting a dog related to my work, and I lost sight of my own personal wants. It made me realise that if work is the main influencing factor, I can always find a solution and juggle my schedule. Now that I'm in my late twenties, I'm choosing a more settled lifestyle and there's no reason why the dog I've always wanted shouldn't be part of that.'

To recap, the Method explained
What's the decision?

Whatever decision you are facing, turn it into a question and pose it to yourself. Make sure you get the question right and phrase it as clearly and simply as possible. This will put distance between you and the problem you are facing, so you can get beyond the haze of anxiety and difficulty you are trying to avoid. This forces you to see your problem as a question which you must answer and therefore forces a decision.

For example, Inès, who has been thinking about this question for a while, had come to see it as a decision only one way – getting a dog – whereas in fact continuing with the status quo can also be framed as a decision, a decision *not* to get a dog. It forced Inès to think of her problem as 'Should I get a dog or continue living without a dog?'. It makes you see both options as choices you make. After all, no decision is also a decision.

Why is this decision important?

Not all decisions can or should be taken through this process. The most important thing to ask yourself is whether this decision will impact your life in, say, ten years' time. This is not a kind of 'butterfly' impact, where we appreciate that any change in direction of anything can trigger a chain of events, doors sliding differently, in a complex and interconnected world. Rather, we are seeking the kind of impacts that we can foresee, connections by which we can make sense of the narratives of our lives.

Asking 'why does it matter?' can be a useful filter for all sorts of decisions which may be holding our lives up by taking up more than their fair share of mental angst. Take elective surgery, for example, which can cover everything from minor wrinkle elimination to preventative bypass surgery. If you are considering a relatively minor cosmetic surgery procedure, ask yourself whether it will impact your life in ten years' time. If you feel it will, unless your career prospects somehow depend on having this surgery (for example, if you are a model and your job depends on your physical appearance) then perhaps you need to re-evaluate your expectations of the outcome of the surgery. An over-optimistic belief in the wide and positive impact of cosmetic surgery points to a psychological malaise well beyond a minor physical concern. In other words, becoming less wrinkly or having a breast enhancement is unlikely to improve your career, financial or social prospects over the long term except in very particular cases.

By the way, take careful note of your response to the question 'why does it matter?', as your answer will provide a useful foundation for the later stage in the process when you are considering all the different areas this decision might impact.

Long-term questions that have a five-to-ten year fallout often relate to one of a list of key life spheres. Consider your problem and decide which key life sphere it falls into. It is likely that it can be fitted into one of the following:

- Career
- Pet ownership
- Having children
- Education
- Elective surgery
- Location
- Property
- Financial investments
- Living together
- Having a relationship

While your problem may be more unusual and lie outside these parameters, they will hopefully be useful in allocating a life area to your problem. More often than not, even if your problem is obscure, it will boil down to one of these key areas.

Think about why this decision is important to you. Why are you struggling to make it? What is the complexity of the question which has resulted in you using this book to help you reach a conclusion?

This part of the process is important in labelling the area of your life your choice will affect: clearly in all of these major life areas the outcome of your decision will have an important impact on your future life and future self. For example, Inès knew straightaway that her problem came under the life area of pet ownership. She then wrote down broad spheres which the outcome of her decision would affect: working life, travel, social life, personal life, leisure time, finances and health. When you consider your question carefully, you will inevitably find the impacts to be broader than you first realised. To help, we have provided a list of the areas which are likely to be impacted by decisions in each of the life spheres, see the Appendix for a list to start you off. If your decision falls outside of one of these spheres, then find the closest spheres and use the list of life areas which might be affected as a prompt.

Once you have the list of areas, think very carefully about all the ways in which the outcome of your decision would affect these areas of your life. Be brutal with yourself. What are the positive and negative consequences of your decision? Imagine the worst (and best) cases. Try to be as objective as possible. Look at Chapter 6 again if you want to remind yourself why that is a good idea.

When we discussed with Inès how a pet would affect her social life, in the best case her new canine friend would improve it, expanding and diversifying her social circle to include fellow dog owners. She also might see more of her current friends as they would be more keen to visit with the added attraction of a puppy. Conversely, in the worst case she would be unable to go on weekend trips to see her friends in London, she wouldn't be able to stay overnight with friends and she thought it would limit her ability to find a boyfriend.

While this may seem ruthless, expanding on your list is an important step in imagining the future. You can't plan for the future if you shy away from what 'may be'. Go through each and every part of your life your decision may affect and write down all the ways this could be affected. This is also a helpful part of the process as things may emerge you had never considered. For example, Inès hadn't fully appreciated that she wouldn't be able to make frequent weekend trips to see her friends further South but also realised, through chatting about it, that there were ways around this, such as driving down or even taking the dog with her on the train. The problems which seemed impossible to negotiate became manageable and even solvable when she thought about them. She said the very act of turning this into a process made it far easier to gain some useful distance from the issue.

The superdriver, further explained

In order to create your four future scenarios, you need to draw up your x- and y- axes. On the horizontal x-axis will be the two possible outcomes of the question you drew up at the beginning of this process. Write these two outcomes at opposite ends of the x-axis. For example, if the question were whether to buy a house or remain renting, on the far left end of the x-axis you would write 'Buy a House' – one of the possible outcomes. And at the far right-hand end of the x-axis, you would write 'Stay Renting' or 'Don't Buy a House'.

The next stage is deciding which factor is the most important in making your decision – this will be the variable on the y-axis. Now this is a little more complicated. Looking at your list of variables, it is the one which is entirely independent of the outcome of the decision you must make. For Inès, it was time as determined by her career – this would vary regardless of whether she bought a dog as she worked in the unpredictable field of journalism. The other factors, such as her health and her social life, were dependent on the outcome of her decision.

There may be occasions where you have more than one possible driver which could go on the y-axis. In this case, you will have to think carefully to decide which is the most important but also the most uncertain. It didn't happen for Inès, but you may see on reflection that one of the remaining drivers is independent of the decision but also constant, in so far as it is not directly affected by the decision but is something which must be factored into any scenario in the same way. We can say these are *independent and constant*, important but certain. If oil prices were the 'independent and constant' driver under discussion, for example, this is not to say that oil prices will not *change*, but rather that they will be a constant factor affecting all scenarios similarly. It's a more complicated aspect of the process, which we will look at in a bit more detail below in Duncan's case study.

The final y-axis which you choose will be independent and variable – these are considerations which will alter importantly, but this alteration is not the result of the outcome of the decision. Instead, this factor has the potential to change the nature of your outcomes.

Once you've figured out which is the most important – and independent – factor in your decision, label the y-axis with the two extremes.

The four scenarios

OK, so now that you have both a diagram to complete and a fairly exhaustive list of possible consequences, the next stage is imagining – as vividly as you can – your future as determined by the two variables which define it. This is where your list of impacts comes into use again. For each of them, consider what your life would look like. Again, it's really important to be as graphic as possible, especially in the worst cases when it's tempting to ignore how life could be. Try to describe the situation as objectively as possible, describe yourself as if in the third person. Seek out those factors or outcomes that you'd rather not think about but which could affect your situation importantly.

What to do next

This is the balancing part – does the worst case of either side outweigh the best cases of the other side? This would make it obvious which outcome is preferable. If even the worst case of one option is better than the best and worst cases of the other option, then it is clear which path you should take to ensure most happiness and satisfaction in your future life.

However, sometimes the choice is not clear-cut. The point of this method is to mentally trace and envisage the possible, and indeed most likely, outcomes of your decision. This process serves as some defence against the pangs of regret which we can all experience when we make ill-informed or uninformed decisions. Too often we don't dedicate the time we should to thinking about 'If...': the why and the wherefore of our choices. This process allows you to take charge of your choices and make the right decisions for your future.

When not to use futurescaping

There are some cases when this process is not appropriate. We realised, as we tried and failed with several of our very accommodating case studies, that where we are looking at wholly emotional questions, such as how a couple resolves competing emotional needs, this kind of process falls down. It is not suitable for questions which are wholly dependent on emotional impulses or philosophical differences. It can't tell you whether you should keep going out with him/her, whether you will ever feel emotionally secure in that relationship, or whether you should have another child although one of you is against it. For two individuals in a relationship, no breakdown of factors or infinite number of drawn-up scenarios can decide if that relationship is really worth pursuing, or can resolve a battle of wills around an emotional issue.

This is another reason why thinking through why this decision is important to you is a vital step. This is the point at which those questions which have a long-term impact but are wholly emotionally or romantically motivated will be filtered out.

Before you demand your money back, I would like to point out that anatomising and solving the problems of romantic love is foxing some of the best. For example, Dan Ariely, a behavioural economics superstar, has turned his psychologist's gaze towards online dating and the disappointed rump of people who have failed to meet their match online despite the ever-more sophisticated Internet models designed to help people find love. He suggests that the disappointment stems from the fact that 'people, unlike many commodities available for purchase online, are experience goods: Daters wish to screen potential romantic partners by experiential attributes (such as sense of humor or rapport), but online dating Web sites force them to screen by searchable attributes (such as income or religion)'[87].

Moved by the plight of a lonely colleague down a university corridor, Professor Ariely has been continuing his research into online dating and, rumour has it, is soon to be publishing more on the subject. However, those of us who have a particular, urgent interest in sussing out this online dating business and finding out what is love, anyway, should perhaps consider looking offline at the same time. As a recent *Guardian* article pointed out, approaching the whole issue of dating by talking about economies of scale and algorithms ensuring utility maximisation 'explains

87   Jeana Frost, Zoë Chance, Michael Norton and Dan Ariely (2008), 'People are Experience Goods: Improving Online Dating with Virtual Dates', *Journal of Interactive Marketing*. Vol. 22, No. 1: 51-61.

why so many behavioural economists spend Saturday nights getting intimate with single-portion lasagnes'[88].

So futurescaping cannot work for love and romantic questions, or issues where something is essentially a battle of wills between two individuals. It could help you consider whether you should be in a relationship *at all*, but it cannot determine whether you should be in a relationship with a particular individual, unless you are truly only taking rational, practical considerations into account for your decision (in which case I would suggest this is not a question about love). Since one of the main benefits of the scenario planning process is gaining objectivity, you must be able to, to some degree, take yourself (temporarily) out of the equation. With relationships, this is close to impossible.

If the decision can be genuinely and sensibly reframed as a rational question rather than a mainly emotional one, then the process can work. For example, if you want to know whether you should keep going out with x or not, and x, by the way, is considering moving to Australia, that is mainly an emotional question. However, if it turns out that x is definitely moving to Australia (with or without you) then you could sensibly have a go at the futurescaping process with the question as to whether you should move to Australia or not, with x just being a factor on the side, as it were. You could only futurescape it this way if you were certain you could set aside the emotion and focus on the rational whilst you are building your scenarios.

Case Study: John

So now hopefully the process is beginning to make some sense, and you already have a decision or two in mind you might have a go at futurescaping. To get more familiar with the process, let's go through John's case study.

Background

John is in his mid-thirties and has worked for the past ten years at an international credit assessment firm managing client accounts. He is finding his current job tedious and insufficiently stimulating. He would like to establish a consultancy for film and television set location, specialising in period dramas. John has well-established connections in this field through friends. However, he is worried by the risk involved in such a transition as he would be giving up the financial security of his current job to create a start-up. John lives with his long-term partner who is also in full-time employment.

The question

'Should I stay in my current field or set up my own business in a new field?'

Why is this decision important to John?

He feels trapped in a job which he doesn't find fulfilling. He sees a clear and attractive alternative to his current career, but he is risk-averse and conscious that he inhabits an age of economic uncertainty.

Which 'life sphere' does this problem fit into?
Career.

We discussed what areas John thought were relevant to a change in this life sphere.

Impact list – list of drivers
- Time – Work/life balance
- External recognition
- Salary
- Intellectual stimulation
- Health of national economy

The following diagram summarises how John expressed his feelings on the subject of changing career. It depicts not only how such a change would affect his finances and lifestyle but also the emotional and psychological impacts such a change would bring about, for example, intellectual stimulation and external recognition. John was also aware of the fact that the health of the national economy could have a big impact on whether now is a good time to become an entrepreneur and, specifically, if clients would have appetite or budget for his services.

Salary
- This will vary hugely with decision. On a reasonable income at the moment – stable. Changing career will inevitably entail more financial risk and will have to accept an initial drop in income
- Not materialistic – huge salary not a concern or motivating factor

Time – Work/Life Balance
- Likes 'to have time to live'
- Time will be limited in new business but long term will have more control over time
- May have to make short-term sacrifices with travel, holidays, etc. to invest time in new company
- Currently, has good free time but overwhelming feelings of stagnation
- Should be able to maintain work/life balance to same level as current. If he wants to spend more time on his new venture, it will be enjoyable

Should I stay in my current job or set up a business in a new field?
Career

External Recogntion
- Not very concerned May receive more recognition for starting something new and different

Intellectual Stimulation
- Finds current job and work environment uninspiring
- Sense of intellectual stagnation or decline in stultifying atmosphere
- The prospect of employing his interests in his professional life is very attractive

Health of National Economy
- Will vary and changes will be beyond his control. Unpredictability will determine the success of new company. If he stays in his old job, he will most likely be relatively unaffected
- In current job has relative security as last-in, first-out shields him – has been there a long time
- In worst case scenario, the new company will open during recession and struggle to find clients, therefore greatly reducing income
- However, there are no dependants so maintaining a steady income is less of a concern. His partner also has a full-time job, so they still can pay the bills

Figure 14

Which is the most important and independent factor?

For John, it was then fairly easy to see that salary, work/life balance, external recognition and intellectual stimulation would be driven by whether or not he decided to stay in his current job or set up his own business. Thus it soon became apparent that the health of the national economy just by elimination was the most important driver, and was the superdriver. It would determine whether the new business would sink or swim.

So John's x- and y-axis looked like this:

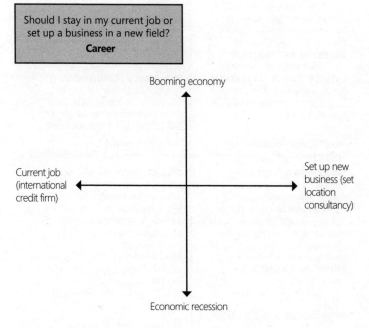

Figure 15

John went on to imagine what his life would be like in each of the scenarios.

Should I stay in my current job or set up a business in a new field?
Career

Booming economy

SALARY: Pay is better
TIME BALANCE: More free time as promotion means PA and more flexible hours. More time to travel and pursue hobbies. More responsibility but fewer working hours due to seniority
EXTERNAL RECOGNITION: Promotion as reward
INTELLECTUAL STIMULATION: Still finding work dull and seeks change. More people on the team to work with

SALARY: Relatively good financial rewards
TIME BALANCE: Have a company with direct employees. Spend most of time at the office. Less time for personal life but better time as much happier in professional life. Partner understanding. Some friends less understanding of reduced social time
EXTERNAL RECOGNITION: Recognised company in the field. Have an international client base. Prestige of owning the investment
INTELLECTUAL STIMULATION: High job satisfaction

Current job ← → **Set up business**

SALARY: Stable. Good benefits – medical, etc. Pay still good relative to lean start-up returns
TIME BALANCE: Job market and career generally less secure, but field not hugely affected by recession. Has seniority so unlikely to lose job. Good work/life balance still intact
EXTERNAL RECOGNITION: Ease of promotion if opportunity arose, but less likely in current climate
INTELLECTUAL STIMULATION: Work dull and boring. Searching for fulfilment

SALARY: Reduced income but still enough money coming from partner's salary. Enough clients to keep going due to good product. Costs managed through fewer direct employees. Options are plugging away or falling back on transferrable skills
TIME BALANCE: Working hours still long but more of a struggle. No PA. More stress from financial challenges and effort required to keep business going. Hung up on winning new business all the time
EXTERNAL RECOGNITION: Some recognition due to good product
INTELLECTUAL STIMULATION: Far better than old job

Economic recession

Figure 16

John's view

'This really made me think seriously about what I *want* to do, rather than what I'm trying to get away from. It also made me think about the issue of someone reluctant to make the initial leap for fear, when it seems so straightforward that they should make the leap. I think looking ten years hence is great: it helps with the visualisation and it's that process that is the tool that helps you. However, there's a huge gap between now and then which makes it seem less real in a way (which I guess also actually helps the exercise). Perhaps doing another, secondary exercise looking six months hence rather than ten years would help focus the mind on what you need to do to ensure:

1. you have planned well;

2. you know what you need to do in the first few months to get your project up and running;

3. (and this seems quite important) you have back-up plans in case having made your decision, for whatever reason you decide not to pursue the project.'

Case Study: Tom

So that's John sorted. Let's speed through one more straightforward example, Tom.

Background

When we spoke to Tom, he had recently finished an MPhil in International Relations at Oxford. He is an American citizen who had completed his first degree in the United States before moving to the UK to complete his master's degree. He has no dependants and is trying to decide whether to pursue a career in the US State Department or in management consultancy.

The question

Should I work for the US State Department or for a management consultancy firm?

Why is this decision important to Tom?

He is under pressure from peers and conscious that he must make a decision about which career path to pursue. There are some similarities about the two options and he is attracted to both paths, yet there are factors which differ in important ways. Tom wants to have status in his career and is trying to marry this with his desire for intellectual fulfilment. He has not considered fully the possibilities both career paths afford as it seems an overwhelming process.

Which 'life sphere' does this problem fit into?
Career.

We then discussed what areas would be affected by a change in this life sphere.

Impact list – list of drivers
- Job security
- Remuneration
- Travel
- Intellectual fulfilment
- Working life
- Status

From a macro factors point of view, Tom also considered the implications of broad changes in business and government, the two sectors he was considering. Political factors could have a big effect on his career prospects in government. What if a new President were to be elected who differed drastically in ideology from Tom? Tom has a professional attitude and said he is eager to serve his country but he is also passionate about politics. Would it be too difficult to work under a government whose priorities he didn't support?

Travel
- Tom would like to travel as much as possible in the next 10-15 years (for business or leisure)
- Both jobs will involve travel, but State Department might provide travel to interesting locales vs corporate facilities
- Consultancy schedule would leave little time for personal travel

Intellectual Fulfilment
- Both career tracks will provide some fulfilment
- State Dept. will be more stimulating and more closely aligned with his interests and education
- Positive feeling of contributing to policy-making on national and international level
- Management consulting less fulfilling at junior level
- However, Tom is attracted to accountabiiity and responsibility from the beginning in consultancy

Working Life
- Management consulting seems exciting and competitive, while governmental works seems more intellectually fulfilling
- Will have to make 10-20 year commitment to government role to see desired career progress

Should I work for the US State Department consultancy?
Career

Job security
- Tom wants job security in life
- Feels both jobs will provide security, perhaps State Department slightly more as is public sector
- Both sectors would be affected in a recession

Status
- Both have status among his peers, however, government has more associated prestige
- Unsure about lifestyle and social culture associated with consultancy
- Unsure about which peer group he would have most in common with
- Once absorbed in either system, he feels he could take on values and adapt to culture around him, so could find peer approval and recognition

Remuneration
- Would like financial security and the ability to maintain a comfortable lifestyle
- Both have high earning potential, but consultancy has a faster career track and higher earning potential at a junior level
- Higher salary in consultancy likely but might come with unreasonable working hours
- State Dept. has lower salary but steady career progression and promotion structure with high earning potential at the top. More expenses covered so fewer outgoings

Figure 17

Which is the most important and independent factor?

As Tom worked through, he realised that all of the drivers except for status could be framed as functions of the decision. The State Department would offer better job security but less remuneration. Consultancy would offer a more hectic working lifestyle but that would be offset by greater salary. The quality of intellectual fulfilment and the type of travel would be a function of the decision either way.

We talked a bit more about this concept of status. Tom had a definite idea that he wanted to do well and to be seen to be doing so, but paradoxically had a rather vague idea of what that actually meant. We explored further and realised that what he meant by status was whether he was doing well in any particular job. We recognised that to some extent, the scope for doing well, for career advancement, would be impacted by the health of the sector in general – no money, fewer openings at a senior level, fewer opportunities to progress. It made sense to have the y-axis as 'doing well' as Tom himself described it, his version of the status driver.

This is the initial diagram we came up with before it was filled in and illustrated according to the feelings towards various drivers:

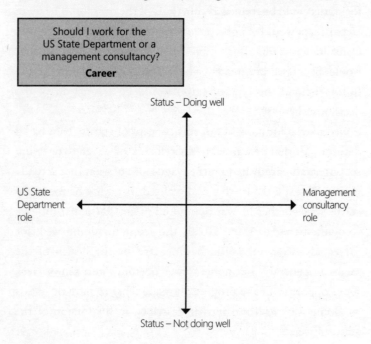

Figure 18

Status – doing well personally in a healthy sector – was clearly the most important factor in determining Tom's decision, as it would have a major impact on his lifestyle and happiness. This is what the scenario diagram looked like once it had been completed:

Should I work for the
US State Department or a
management consultancy?
Career

Status – Doing Well

WORKING LIFE: Moderate work/life balance
JOB SECURITY: Reached the zenith of state positions – assistant secretary Strong government with lots of funding
FULFILMENT: In a position where his input makes a difference. Stimulation is at a high level
TRAVEL: A lot of travel on government time and expenses
REMUNERATION: Not as high as top consultancy job
STATUS: Interesting and like-minded peers. Prestige high

WORKING LIFE: Not as much time to see family and friends as would like
JOB SECURITY: Been there 10-15 years. To a large degree, control your own destiny
FULFILMENT: Specialized in one sector most likely. Running own practice – or will be soon
TRAVEL: Less travel. Travel is about retaining client relationships
REMUNERATION: Pay very high
STATUS: Prestige of experience and wealth

US State Deparment role ←———→ **Management consultancy role**

WORKING LIFE: More free time, though works a lot out of feeling of job insecurity
JOB SECURITY: Government smaller, limited funding due to economic bust scenario. Fewer people able to climb the ladder to promotion
FULFILMENT: Restructured department – entirely top down organisation. Even though has been there for a long time, his input isn't meaningful
TRAVEL: Very limited expenses and travel
REMUNERATION: Salary lower than worst case consulting scenario, but good pension
STATUS: Low status and prestige in this scenario

WORKING LIFE: Spending a lot of time at work, but not as much as boom consultancy scenario
JOB SECURITY: Still have jobs but top tier companies have been swallowed. Much has been automated
FULFILMENT: At a smaller firm. Time invested but still very bored. Not sufficient intellectual reward. Job as a means to an end
TRAVEL: Some money and time to travel as a way to gain fulfilment
REMUNERATION: Good salary but doesn't know what to do with it
STATUS: Low-Medium status and prestige levels

Status – Not doing well

Figure 19

The outcome

This is an unusual case as to some extent the variable on the y-axis is within Tom's control. Should there be changes on the economic climate, these would determine the situation in ways beyond his influence. However, diligence and application of skills could lead to him determining his own professional advancement either in a management consultancy firm or within the federal government.

In the end, Tom decided to take a role he was offered with a management consultancy in New York.

Tom's view

'I thought that this was an extremely instructive exercise for me personally, and would be for readers of your book. To put a job seeker or someone who is considering changing careers into the black and white 'A vs B' scenario is crucial. Even though it may force a decision, if you have properly laid out pros and cons as well as best case/worst case scenarios, it should be extremely beneficial to those attempting to do their own scenario planning.

'At first glance, thinking about how my decisions today might effect my career/personal life ten or 15 years down the road is certainly daunting and intimidating. However, I really believe this process makes that decision appear, at least on paper, to be extremely rational and grounded. I think the process you have developed can be calming for those facing uncertainty.'

Let's move on now to some slightly more complex examples. One of the things which can complicate the process is trying to make a decision which affects more than one person. As long as this isn't a purely emotionally driven decision where two people are just going to have to battle it out emotionally or philosophically, there is no reason why different drivers can't be taken into account and explored. To illustrate, let's take the example of Joanna and Ben, who were trying to work out whether or not to relocate to the Netherlands as a couple.

Case study: Joanna and Ben
Background
Ben works for a brand consultancy and has an attractive offer to go out to Amsterdam and set up the Netherlands office. Joanna is an experienced yoga instructor but has no work secured in Amsterdam. In London, she works for a well-established yoga company.

The question
Should they relocate to the Netherlands together?

Why is this decision important to them?
Well settled in London, moving to Amsterdam will mean major upheaval for both of them. It is likely to have a big impact on many areas of their lives, taking them both along new trajectories.

They are in their late twenties, unmarried and don't have children, but may consider kids in the future. They currently rent a flat in Islington, a trendy area in London.

Which 'life sphere' does this problem fit into?

The life sphere is about location. They identified the following life areas as driving or relevant to the decision:

- Career progression
- Financial health
- Children
- Home life
- Travel/Leisure
- Social engagement

Ben and Joanna also considered the bigger factors that could have an impact on their scenarios. The recent societal focus on health concerns and a mainstreaming of yoga practice made Joanna's career choice seem fairly stable. The fact that Joanna and Ben were unmarried, while it could be problematic in some societies, would be acceptable in the Netherlands.

We went through the areas in detail.

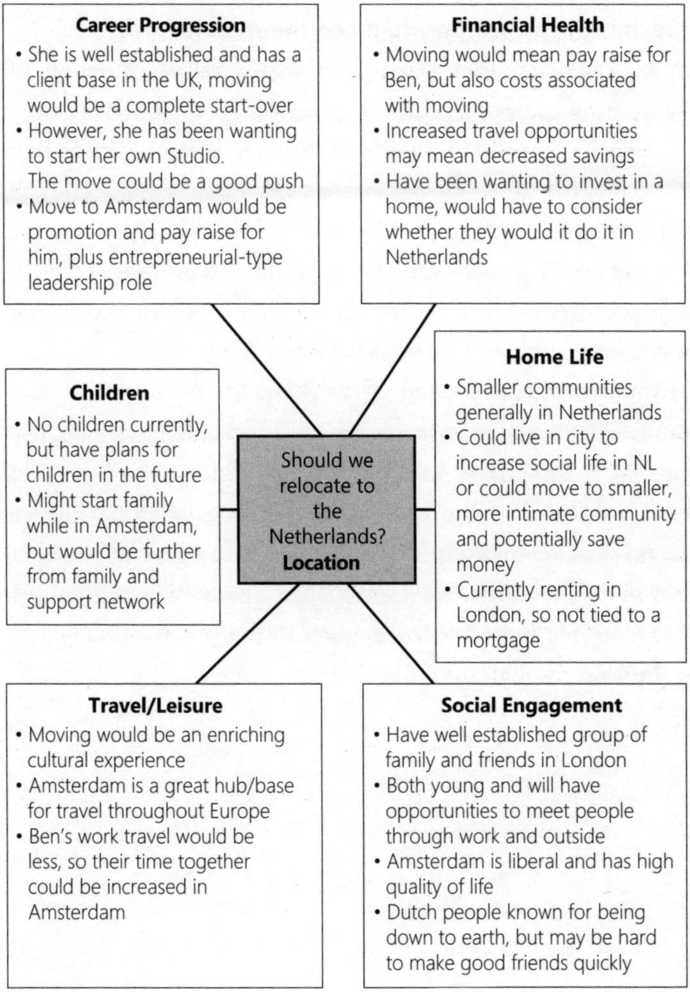

Career Progression
- She is well established and has a client base in the UK, moving would be a complete start-over
- However, she has been wanting to start her own Studio. The move could be a good push
- Move to Amsterdam would be promotion and pay raise for him, plus entrepreneurial-type leadership role

Financial Health
- Moving would mean pay raise for Ben, but also costs associated with moving
- Increased travel opportunities may mean decreased savings
- Have been wanting to invest in a home, would have to consider whether they would it do it in Netherlands

Children
- No children currently, but have plans for children in the future
- Might start family while in Amsterdam, but would be further from family and support network

Should we relocate to the Netherlands? **Location**

Home Life
- Smaller communities generally in Netherlands
- Could live in city to increase social life in NL or could move to smaller, more intimate community and potentially save money
- Currently renting in London, so not tied to a mortgage

Travel/Leisure
- Moving would be an enriching cultural experience
- Amsterdam is a great hub/base for travel throughout Europe
- Ben's work travel would be less, so their time together could be increased in Amsterdam

Social Engagement
- Have well established group of family and friends in London
- Both young and will have opportunities to meet people through work and outside
- Amsterdam is liberal and has high quality of life
- Dutch people known for being down to earth, but may be hard to make good friends quickly

Figure 20

Which is the most important and independent factor?

We realised that to some extent, all of the drivers were functions of the decision except for Joanna's career progression (Ben's career, as it was the centre of the main question, was obviously a function of the x-axis). Does it matter that the y-axis was just about one half of the couple? No, because they were contemplating this move together and both were sure that they didn't want to try living in separate cities. While the move was attractive for Ben, the biggest uncertainty hung over Joanne's future.

Joanna had had enough of working for other people and wanted to set up her own yoga studio, possibly in a niche like children's yoga. However, while she was fairly sure she could manage this in the UK where she has contacts, clients and 'knows the ropes', she was completely unsure if this was viable for her elsewhere. Thus their y-axis was Joanna successfully setting up a yoga studio or Joanna without a new business and struggling to find work.

> Should we relocate to the Netherlands?
> **Location**

Joanna – own yoga studio

CAREER PROGRESSION: Ben's stays the same. Joanna well connected to start studio. Joanna highly motivated

FINANCIAL HEALTH: New business is initially more about investment than profit

CHILDREN: May not be the best time to start a family

HOME LIFE: Home life stays relatively the same. Some emotional pressure as they've stayed in UK for her

SOCIAL ENGAGEMENT: Remain near London friends and family. Nothing too new

TRAVEL/LEISURE: Joanna's time limited due to new studio, but she makes own hours

CAREER PROGRESSION: Both are motivated and fulfilled. A lot of time and energy in new jobs

FINANCIAL HEALTH: High income due to Ben's promotion and popularity of new yoga studio. More money to spend

CHILDREN: Limited time, but more financial resources for help if they decide to have a baby

HOME LIFE: More time together as a couple due to less travel and Joanna setting own hours. Able to rent larger flat so family and friends can visit

SOCIAL ENGAGEMENT: Loosening of ties to London friends, but more money to visit UK. Smaller city, less to do

TRAVEL/LEISURE: Greater time for travel, leisure, culture and exercise.

Stay in London ← → **Move to Amsterdam**

CAREER PROGRESSION: Joanna unfulfilled, feels a status difference between Ben and her. Feels little control over her timetable. Feels Ben's friends look down on her. Ben refused new role – will this mean plateau or less-favoured status in company?

FINANCIAL HEALTH: Money is same as before

CHILDREN: Joanna would like to adjust her schedule, but worries about giving up her career

HOME LIFE: Time together limited due to evening and morning yoga classes. Joanna feels disconnected from Ben's life

SOCIAL ENGAGEMENT: Remain near London friends and family.

TRAVEL/LEISURE: Ben away a lot with work. Able to do some travel together

CAREER PROGRESSION: Joanna working part-time for a studio

FINANCIAL HEALTH: Joanna feels she can't contribute financially as she would like. Ben's promotion means money is ok.

CHILDREN: May be a good time to think about having a baby as Joanna has a natural break in her career and money is okay

HOME LIFE: Not as much resources for setting up life in Amsterdam. Joanna spends much time alone. Emotional pressure that they've moved for him

SOCIAL ENGAGEMENT: Ben is building a new network and feels integrated. Joanna feels somewhat left behind and isolated. Since they don't have kids, she can't tap into mummy network

TRAVEL/LEISURE: More time to travel together, continental Europe

Joanna – no new business or struggling business

Figure 21

They discussed the scenarios carefully. There were some uncomfortable moments, for example when they were considering what life might be like if Joanna's work didn't take off in Amsterdam. What happened in the end?

Should we relocate to the Netherlands? **Location**

The outcome for Joanna and Ben:
- Realised need to do proper research to test viability of Joanna's business idea
- Realised how much both love travelling. There's something about the appeal of the new which moved both of them
- They decided to go as soon as possible to Amsterdam to seriously check out what living there (rather than holidaying) might be like
- Concerned both will regret it if they don't make the move
- Assuming Amsterdam checks out ok, both decided they want to make the move with the explicit aim of Joanna setting up a studio there

Figure 22

Joanna and Ben's views

'We found this really useful. We had both got quite emotional about the potential move, and it was turning into an increasingly urgent issue that both of us were sidestepping. It was great because it made us confront head on the issue that if we were going to go, we would be putting Ben's career over mine.' (Joanna)

'It was surprising that such an ostensibly rational approach helped us deal with the emotional stuff. We know we want to be together long-term so we should be making decisions with that in mind. Making Joanna's studio a reality is now a project for both of us. We've now got a plan of action to follow: we need to sort out Joanna's business plan, spend some time in Amsterdam and if it all checks out, off we go!' (Ben)

Case Study: Viv and Joel

Sometimes dealing with two people in this process can get more complicated, although this is not a reason to be put off. Let's take one more couple, Viv and Joel.

Background

Viv and Joel are a young couple thinking of buying a home. Joel is currently in his fifth year studying medicine, and will become a junior doctor next year. Viv has just finished her MBA and is looking for jobs in the City. They met at university, love each other and want to get married at some point. They are both based in London and are trying to decide whether to move in with friends and live separately or buy a property together. They know they don't want to be 'the couple' in a house otherwise filled with single sharers. This decision is complicated as the job market is uncertain and they are under pressure from peers and family members who feel they would be unwise to invest at such a young age.

The question

Should we move into separate rented houses with friends or buy a house together?

Why is the question important?

This is a major life decision which will affect not only where they live, but their social lives, personal relationship and finances. There are additional complications due to the uncertainty of the job market and the disapproval of their parents. The impact area of 'job market' was also somewhat related to the value of their recent university degrees. Current debates on education mean that degrees could become less valued and that on-the-job training could gain new importance, although ultimately Viv and Joel felt relatively secure that their degrees would still be valued in business and medicine respectively.

Which life area does this fit into?

Property ownership/Living.

Which areas of their lives will the decision affect?

This diagram shows the complex interaction of factors in the decision-making process. Viv and Joel had been understandably overwhelmed by competing views from all around, and many different issues. Visualising these drivers helped them to compartmentalise the various issues this question raised:

Domestic Life
- Very much like married couple if they move in together
- More of a student lifestyle if living with friends
- Possible arguments over chores. More stressful than having disagreements with friends

Work/Life Balance
- If the need for money was very acute this would most likely make work the more dominant factor
- This could upset the balance and put strain on the relationship

Job Market/Economic Health
- Would they be able to keep up with mortgage payments if there was a double-dip recession?
- If job market healthy, both will be earning money. Both well qualified but job market is saturated
- Could result in very little time together
- If living together, they would be able to support each other during tough time
- Living together may exacerbate the stress of job hunting

Emotional Impact
- Strong sense of nesting/domesticity
- Is this premature for people in their early twenties? Possible regret routine/commitment
- Instability of living with friends – don't want to carry on with student lifestyle
- Greater sense of stability living with partner
- Aim to get married – are very committed to each other so why not start now?

Career Path
- Viv may take jobs due to pressure of initially being main earner. Joel will not be a junior doctor until next year
- Both will have jobs taking them out of the home a lot

Relationship with Family
- Possible becomes strained if they go against the wishes of the family
- In reality, family will probably support their decision

Location & Commuting Time and Distance
- Will have to live in inconvenient location (not central). High commuting costs
- Location will affect social life
- Possibly have to live in less safe and secure area where property prices are lower
- Tiring to have to commute on top of medicine's anti-social working hours

Should we move into separate rented houses with friends or buy a house together?
Property Ownership

Financial Responsibility/ Finance Management
- Have been left inheritance – enough for a deposit. Want to invest wisely
- Burden of financial obligations
- Positive sense of maturity and adulthood
- May affect careers – inclined to take jobs quickly and not necessarily make best decisions due to financial necessity
- No space for a lodger. One bed flat at top end of budget
- Can't just move home or move out if they don't like it
- Feel that renting is wasting money – throwing money away

Social Life
- If living with friends, there is ready-made social life
- If living only with partner, less likely to socialise
- May live less centrally; therefore may become isolated from social circle
- Possibly will develop new friends in community
- Small flat – can't invite people over to socialise

Figure 23

It was tricky and complicated, but eventually we got there by systematically going through the list of life areas and discussing each one.

How did we work out the superdriver from all of this lot? Well, actually it wasn't that hard. As we went through each of them, we realised that they were all pretty much a function of the main question, would be shaped by the decision in one clear direction or another. This was the case for everything except the job market (and, by implication, their economic health), which they felt in both of their sectors would be dependent on the overall state of the economy.

So, building on all of that discussion about the different impact areas, this is what their scenario matrix looked like:

> Should we move into separate rented houses with friends or buy a house together?
> **Location**

Good job market/boom economy

FINANCIAL RESPONSIBILITY: Able to save money for future home investment
SOCIAL LIFE: Social life is good
RELATIONSHIP: Don't spend as much time together alone as they would like
LOCATION/COMMUTE: Both in fairly good location
WORK/LIFE BALANCE: Both are working a lot, but have built-in social life in their off time
EMOTIONAL IMPACT: Progression in their careers partially compensates for less 'mature' relationship
DOMESTIC LIFE: Flats are not as tidy as they'd like.
CAREER PATH: Both feel secure in their career path

FINANCIAL RESPONSIBILITY: Making good money, most goes toward mortgage and home maintenance
SOCIAL LIFE: See friends less often, tend to spend time at new home or with new neighbours
RELATIONSHIP: Both work a lot, but living together opens up time
LOCATION/COMMUTE: Longer commute since could not afford central location
WORK/LIFE BALANCE: Tilting towards work
EMOTIONAL IMPACT: Would like more time together, but happy to be progressing their careers and relationship
DOMESTIC LIFE: Feels like being married; they feel it is a good test, enjoy doing up home
CAREER PATH: Both are progressing their careers as hoped for

Rent with friends ←————————————→ **Buy house together**

FINANCIAL RESPONSIBILITY: Glad to keep costs down as money is tight
SOCIAL LIFE: Lots of time for social activities, but little money. Feels a bit like uni all over again
RELATIONSHIP: Strained under the pressure of job hunting and living apart
LOCATION/COMMUTE: Living fairly centrally, but can't afford the lifestyle that goes with it
WORK/LIFE BALANCE: More life than work, but constantly looking for jobs
EMOTIONAL IMPACT: Lots of stress individually
DOMESTIC LIFE: Flats are bit run down, they spend time cleaning
CAREER PATH: Both feel insecure in their career paths

FINANCIAL RESPONSIBILITY: Money all goes toward mortgage and home maintenance. Financial stress
SOCIAL LIFE: See less of friends, can't afford to travel into city all the time
RELATIONSHIP: Able to spend lots of time together, but both stressed
LOCATION/COMMUTE: Commute less of an issue, but living far out with little money is isolating.
WORK/LIFE BALANCE: Don't have work, but don't feel balanced
EMOTIONAL IMPACT: Feel as though they are 'playing house' too young
DOMESTIC LIFE: Can't afford to do up home as they would like
CAREER PATH: Both feel insecure in their career paths. Likely that one of couple will be unemployed. Major emotional stress

Economic recession

Figure 24

The outcome: both Viv and Joel became quite emotional during the futurescaping session, but kept insisting they wanted to keep going and resolve this. When they looked over the scenarios they had created, they both agreed that buying a property now was an overly hasty move, and that there was no need to buy right away. They both said at the time and afterwards that it had been very useful and eye-opening, and they were glad that they had gone through the process.

Viv and Joel's view

'We're really glad we've gone through this. It was definitely worth it. We realise that maybe we were trying to prove something but it makes much more sense to think things through.'

Case Study: Duncan
Background

In all of the case studies we have examined so far, the selection of the y-axis was a relatively straightforward process. All of the candidate drivers bar one were so closely intertwined with the decision and how it was taken that they could effectively be 'collapsed' into the same axis, leaving one outstanding driver to be the superdriver.

However, once you have come up with all of your drivers, it may not always happen that only one is left as the y-axis candidate. What do you do? This is where you are in the similar position to the point in corporate scenario planning when the coffees get refilled and the groups get ready for some hard thinking. It is possible to frame it as (or some would say *reduce* it to) a mathematical question, but even dependency matrices will only get you so far. Ultimately it has to be a subjective decision, usually reached through fairly drawn-out discussion, as to which are the most important and most uncertain drivers.

In the case of individuals futurescaping, this problem is at least halved in so far as the x-axis is set by the decision itself, so there is only one driver to choose. Nonetheless, it does mean that some thinking has to be done to establish what the superdriver is: you still have to work out what is most important and uncertain when it comes to you making this decision. This is an important point to highlight. The issue is not which driver is the most important and uncertain in general, but which is the most important and uncertain *in this context*, as you sit there facing this specific decision.

To illustrate how we might get through this particular complexity, let's take the example of Duncan. Duncan is in his early forties and living in Aberdeen, having spent most of his working life in London. He works as a joiner in a specialist field – building and restoring furniture that uses reclaimed wood. The demand for his work is steady but with a recent popular trend towards vintage and antique interiors, he has seen an increase in the demand for his work. One of the reasons he moved to Aberdeen was to be close to his mum, who is frail. Duncan has previously been a homeowner. However, the house he bought was relatively large for one person, and had a big garden. Feeling overwhelmed by the amount of effort and attention it required to upkeep, he sold it and returned to the rental market. He is now considering buying a house. However, this is a complex decision as not only does it have a long-term impact on his future life, but a negative experience of previous homeownership has left him wary.

The question
Should I buy a house in Aberdeen or continue to rent?

Why is this decision important to Duncan?
Duncan feels increasingly dissatisfied with his living arrangements. While there is no pressing difficulty or problem, renting is leading to feelings of instability. He would like somewhere to feel like home. However, he admits to being somewhat scarred by what he now sees as his previous ill-judged property investment. He also has a number of factors complicating the issue, such as concern for the future health of his mum.

> Do I buy a house in Aberdeen or continue to rent?
> **Property Ownership**

Figure 25

Which life sphere does this problem fit into?
Property ownership.

We then discussed what areas would be impacted by a change in this life sphere.

Impact list – list of drivers

- Career and demand for his work
- Dependants (health of his mum)
- Mobility/travel
- Finances
- State of the housing market
- 'Rootedness'

This is what the initial diagram looked like when Duncan considered the broad areas his decision would affect, and be affected by:

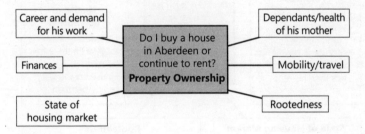

Figure 26

This led to a more detailed version of the diagram once he had considered all of the possible effects on these areas if he were to buy – or not buy – a house in Aberdeen.

Career and Demand for his Work

- Demand for his work is determined by popular taste in interior design
- While demand is currently high as people are favouring a vintage, distressed look, this may lessen if taste swings towards modernity. Then his income will be reduced
- Reduced availability of reclaimed timber due to the recession, fewer houses are being taken down
- Could use other wood such as oak and pine

Mobility/Travel

- If he wants to move around and travel, a house is a big commitment – it will tie him down. Conversely, this will make him happier in his current location as it will give him a sense of stability and rootedness to the community

Finances

- House buying is a very big financial commitment
- Mortgage payments would probably be less than his rent

Do I buy a house in Aberdeen or continue to rent?
Property Ownership

Dependants/ Health of his Mother

- He wants to stay local to be there for his mum
- House buying will be in Aberdeen

State of Housing Market

- Houses are still reasonable to buy in Aberdeen
- Chances are that he could sell off his debt with the house – unlikely to be worse off financially by buying

Rootedness

- He feels better than he used to about house buying – he was previously very reluctant due to his ill-informed choice to buy five years ago.
- If he chose the right house – not a large family property but a modest size – he thinks it would make him very happy

Figure 27

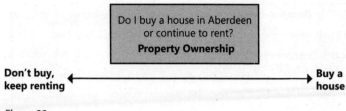

Figure 28

Here's the x-axis. But how would Duncan get to the superdriver?

Which is the most important and independent factor?

In order to get to the superdriver, we went through the initial list of impact areas. The areas of rootedness, finances and travel/mobility were all very closely connected to his housing decision and their outcomes would clearly shift depending on which way he decided. If he bought, he would be more rooted; he would be paying a mortgage, receiving the possible addition of rent from a lodger rather than paying rent himself; and he would be less inclined to go and visit friends down South. Thus we could set these concerns aside for now.

However, this still left Duncan with three possible candidates for the y-axis: the state of the housing market, his mum's dependency on him and the amount of demand there would be for his work based on whether popular tastes turned towards nostalgia or modernity. All of these were undoubtedly important. However, as he talked more about it, we started to realise that when it came to this particular decision there was little uncertainty *for Duncan* regarding the state of the housing market or his mum's health. He had decided to stay in Aberdeen where the property prices seem fairly stable, so he felt the state of the property market didn't really make much difference to his decision. As for his mum's health, that was a constant but unchanging factor. He had already decided he would stay in Aberdeen, whether renting or buying, to be close to her. So whilst, of course, the state of her health is somewhat uncertain, in terms of how it impacts on this particular decision, this is unvarying. Thus, both of these two were no longer candidates for the y-axis, leaving the demand for Duncan's particular joinery skills, which are dependent on popular taste.

It's important to note, though, that both of the 'failed' y-axis candidates had been clouding Duncan's decision. As they are both emotional factors for Duncan, worrying about the housing market and his mum's health had been stopping him even trying to think about the whole decision rationally. Every time he tried to sit down and think about it, these issues clamoured to the surface and turned him elsewhere. It's an excellent reminder of the benefits of futurescaping beyond building scenarios to make a particular decision. The process can help you disentangle the real decision-drivers from the emotional blockages or red herrings.

So Duncan's y-axis was the popular taste for nostalgia vs taste for modernity which he felt would be the most important and most uncertain driver for demand for his line of work.

Once both axes had been drawn and the list of drivers discussed in detail, we were able to construct a series of detailed likely scenarios. The diagram below shows the four most likely future scenarios:

> Do I buy a house in Aberdeen or continue to rent?
> **Property Ownership**

Popular taste for nostalgia = high work demand

LIVING: High monthly rent
SOCIAL: More mobile and free to travel. Less inclined to socialise at home
EMOTIONAL: Least attractive option – just cruising along like last few years. Doesn't feel like home still – if you buy, the house belongs to the bank, but still have a sense of ownership. If you rent, you have to stick to landlord's rules

LIVING: Finds a suitable house. Décor is not to his taste but free to change it. UK has an ethos of restoring properties
CAREER: Would stay in company if offered a better job? Even if worked on his own would want his own home. Job satisfaction
SOCIAL: Would spend more time socialising at home. More keen to have friends round at own place. Going out less to socialise anyway
FINANCIAL: Could take on lodger for extra income
EMOTIONAL: Positive feeling of rootedness in the community

Don't buy, ◄─────────────────────────► **Buy a house**
keep renting

LIVING: Just moved, having to move again.
CAREER: Work life less fulfilling – very repetitive. More commercial, less creative work.
SOCIAL: Less inclined to socialise at home. Less free to travel as you have less money
FINANCIAL: Uncertain prospects
EMOTIONAL: Doesn't feel like home still – if you buy, the house belongs to the bank, but still have sense of ownership. If you rent, you have to stick to landlord's rules. Still just cruising along – very unattractive prospect. Feelings of stagnation

LIVING: House wouldn't be perfect.
CAREER: Work life less fulfilling- very repetitive. More commercial, less creative work
SOCIAL: Would spend more time socialising at home. More keen to have friends round at own place
FINANCIAL: More stress from financial pressures – less disposable income. Could take a lodger
EMOTIONAL: Could feel trapped by house, would miss seeing friends down South (cash constrained)

Popular taste for modern = low work demand

Figure 29

The outcome

By the end of the process, Duncan had clarified that despite his previous negative experience of homeownership he felt very strongly about buying his own house. He identified that he was scared of home buying due to his previous negative experience, but he could alleviate these fears by changing how and what he bought. The prospect of continuing to rent filled him with dread and it became very clear that the feelings of stagnation surrounding renting outweighed the feelings of anxiety associated with purchasing a property. He realised through the process that even the worst-case scenario of house buying was favourable to that of continuing to rent. The process also drew his attention to the financial aspect of his decision. He felt he had not spent a sufficient amount of time calculating costs. Duncan realised that he needed to adopt a far more rational approach and consider his issue in a less emotional way.

Duncan's view

'Laying it all out in a quadrant made me realise that the choice was not 'Buying or Not Buying', but 'Buying or Renting'. I think I had been scared of buying again so not buying was less a choice than a fearful fallback. And it made me think about renting as a choice. I had been thinking about the question in a very emotional way and it was good to have a structured way of analysing the question: not to take all the emotion out of it, but to not let it dominate.'

Let's look at another example where there was more than one possible superdriver. Sarah was battling with whether or not she should try for a second child.

Case study: Sarah

In this case the question making up the x-axis (whether or not to try for a second child) was clearly defined. It was certainly a decision that would matter in five years' time and therefore required careful consideration. Sarah is in her mid-thirties, married, and has a son, Jacob. She has lived in London since her early twenties and has a small restaurant PR firm.

Sarah saw the following as her impact areas when deciding whether having a second child could be a viable possibility for her family:

- Career
- Finances
- Location
- Relationship with children
- Physical Health
- Leisure time/social interaction
- Environment
- Schooling

Having identified these, we then examined the implications of her decision in each of the impact areas.

Sarah's career in restaurant PR is doing well – she has been right in the thick of things representing innovative restaurants and influential chefs all over London. Although she has some anxiety about stepping back from this fast-paced world, she feels her relationships in the industry are strong enough that she can work from home part-time and not become out of touch. However, adding a second child would be a strain on the time she could devote to her career. When she had Jacob, it took her 12 to 18 months to get back to what she felt was a position equal to the one she had prior to her pregnancy. This time around, she would prepare financially and mentally for a six-month break, although in the fast-moving restaurant industry, six months can seem like a lifetime. She is concerned that she will be that bit older and the business market could be more difficult when she's ready to return.

Sarah and her husband have also been considering their future living location as part of the decision to add to their family. For the first time in their marriage, they are wondering if they would be happy to move outside of the city. More space and more affordable housing might be nice, along with more green space. Once the baby gets a bit older, they will need more home space, and Sarah would love to have more outdoor space for the kids. Sarah has always considered herself an urbanite, though, and wonders if she would be bored away from London's culture and excitement.

A second pregnancy could be a stress on Sarah's health, although she had regained any lost fitness first time around running after Jacob as a toddler, and said she would have an incentive to focus on healthy eating and exercise to be a good role model for the kids.

Socially, she worries about Jacob growing up in the city. Although her important relationships (and her husband's) are London-based, it can feel isolating for a child, especially one who is not yet enrolled in school. She wonders if living in a more cohesive neighbourhood or smaller community would help Jacob develop socially. The addition of a brother or sister would also provide the addition of a ready-made playmate for Jacob.

Having a second child would obviously bring additional costs, but Sarah and her husband wonder if these could be at least partially offset by a move outside of central London. She also wonders about the addition of the second child in terms of family dynamic. Will she be adding stress to her marriage? How will Jacob adjust to not being an only child any longer? However, she has always loved the idea of Jacob having a brother or sister and it could, in fact, strengthen the family unit.

Finally, Sarah must consider schooling. In London, state school catchment areas are small, and there is a chance the family would have to relocate to get Jacob into what they saw as a good state school. She and her husband have considered private schooling for Jacob, but the costs are such that a second child would mean state school for both kids.

Here's the summary of our discussion:

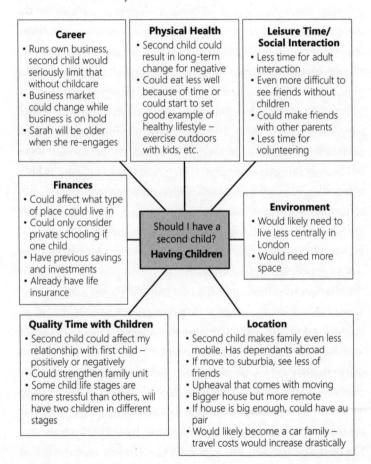

Career
- Runs own business, second child would seriously limit that without childcare
- Business market could change while business is on hold
- Sarah will be older when she re-engages

Physical Health
- Second child could result in long-term change for negative
- Could eat less well because of time or could start to set good example of healthy lifestyle – exercise outdoors with kids, etc.

Leisure Time/ Social Interaction
- Less time for adult interaction
- Even more difficult to see friends without children
- Could make friends with other parents
- Less time for volunteering

Finances
- Could affect what type of place could live in
- Could only consider private schooling if one child
- Have previous savings and investments
- Already have life insurance

Should I have a second child?
Having Children

Environment
- Would likely need to live less centrally in London
- Would need more space

Quality Time with Children
- Second child could affect my relationship with first child – positively or negatively
- Could strengthen family unit
- Some child life stages are more stressful than others, will have two children in different stages

Location
- Second child makes family even less mobile. Has dependants abroad
- If move to suburbia, see less of friends
- Upheaval that comes with moving
- Bigger house but more remote
- If house is big enough, could have au pair
- Would likely become a car family – travel costs would increase drastically

Figure 30

Which is the most important and independent factor?

Sarah then evaluated each of these drivers to determine which was the most important and uncertain in influencing her decision.

Even though she had previously been aware of the importance she placed on location, she did not realise before undertaking the exercise just how much she valued her *central* location.

Although somewhat secondary, Sarah was also aware of larger societal shifts that could affect the way she felt about this decision. She was at a stage in her life when many of her contemporaries were moving out of the city and having children. She admitted that her concepts of feminism and motherhood did play into a certain reluctance about becoming what could be perceived as a suburban 'yummy mummy' type. These concerns were not core for Sarah, but in scenario planning it is good to acknowledge societal factors that could either impact your decision-making or its results.

In a way, the issue of a second child is entangled with the decision to stay in central London or to make a move to the suburbs. Both are likely to have a dramatic influence on the family's life, and the factor of location is really the only candidate for the superdriver, as it is so important to her family's future.

The effect location would have on her lifestyle then became the y-axis. This case is somewhat different from many of the other futurescaping case studies because obviously to a large degree her location is within her family's control. Nonetheless, this was the driver she saw as being most important and was still uncertain. In that way, her scenarios were very clearly defined. In the top-left quadrant she lives in central London and has one child. In the bottom right, she lives in suburbia and has two children, etc. However, the key issue was exploring the effects a second child or relocation would have on her family's life.

Here is the diagram that illustrates the four possible scenarios:

Should I have a second child?
Having Children

Live centrally

FINANCES: No live-in help affordable
PHYSICAL HEALTH: Sarah has time to exercise
LEISURE TIME/SOCIAL INTERACTION: Socialising difficult for Jacob. Sarah has time for hobbies and time with husband and Jacob.
ENVIRONMENT: Fewer groups of kids and friendship opportunities in central London. School might help this for Jacob
LOCATION: Short commute to work but tiny catchment areas for good schools
QUALITY TIME WITH CHILDREN: Low commute time and work schedule means more time with Jacob
CAREER: Career going well
SCHOOLING: Broader range of school choices, but still might require in-city move

FINANCES: Childcare costs even more constrained
PHYSICAL HEALTH: Family exercises together at the weekend
LEISURE TIME/SOCIAL INTERACTION: Companionship for Jacob. Sarah's existing leisure and social time more limited but maintains existing relationships in city
ENVIRONMENT: Extra pressure from space limits
LOCATION: Short commute to work but tiny catchments for good schools
QUALITY TIME WITH CHILDREN: Low commute time but juggling difficult
CAREER: No live-in help = big impact on career. Career tailored around nursery school times
SCHOOLING: Both attending state school so must move closer to good school

No second child ◄—————————————————► **Second child**

FINANCES: Enough money and space for au pair and fulltime childcare. Potentially enough money for private school. More disposable income for travel and hobbies
PHYSICAL HEALTH: Time and space for healthy lifestyle
LEISURE TIME/SOCIAL INTERACTION: Can keep up some relationships with friends and family, but less inclined to travel. Less of a support network
ENVIRONMENT: Less urban leisure, but new options
LOCATION: Possibly beautiful country-side. Need a car
QUALITY TIME WITH CHILDREN: Longer commute for Sarah and her husband, but spend weekends outdoors
CAREER: Sarah setting own hours and working from home half the time.
SCHOOLING: More choice of schools, considering private school for Jacob

FINANCES: Big commuting travel costs and child-care costs offset by lower housing costs
PHYSICAL HEALTH: Less time for maintaining healthy lifestyle
LEISURE TIME/SOCIAL INTERACTION: Existing social relationships become strained
ENVIRONMENT: Enough space for live-in help. New community relationships. Distance from family. Less support network. Less urban leisure, but new options
LOCATION: Possibly beautiful country-side. Need a car
QUALITY TIME WITH CHILDREN: Sarah might work less to mitigate rising childcare costs with two children
CAREER: Lesser impact on work, more flexibility in hours. Less inclination to come to office – working from home space.
SCHOOLING: More choice of state schools in area

Live in suburbia

Figure 31

Through the futurescaping process, Sarah was able to understand that she really needed to plan for the career hit she might take if she had a second child.

In terms of location, she also started to wonder if she was being too black and white in terms of lifestyles of 'city' and 'suburbs.' Perhaps there is something in between that she wasn't able to see and consider before?

If she stayed in very central London, there's no space for live-in help, but she is willing to explore other options, such as a 'mother's help' for mornings when she has important meetings.

She also realised that she was being a bit unrealistic about the relationship between having a second child and the status of her career and lifestyle. She and her husband have to compromise and balance their time already with just Jacob, and in fact it may not be that the work 'doubles' with a second child, but rather she must just think of it in a different way.

Sarah also decided that time with her children, whether with just one child or with two, is of utmost importance to her. Her fear of losing out on her kids' childhoods was far scarier to her than getting behind in her career, which she'd focused on for close to 15 years before Jacob was born.

Futurescaping with Sarah provided a useful and interesting illustration of how deliberately trying to identify and talk through different factors can bring to the surface invisible assumptions which are affecting your logic. Sarah had conflated the idea of having a second child with a move to the suburbs, adding even more weight and confusion to an already laden question. This didn't have to be the case.

Sarah's view

'I realised that location and my career are important to me, but not as important as quality time with my kids. We are fairly sure we do want to have a second child, but only if our careers and lifestyle can support us enjoying quality time together as a family, whether that be in the city or the suburbs.'

Case study: Kat

Our last case study is Kat. We selected her as a case study because she neatly illustrates how *Futurescaping* can untie emotional knots. In Kat's case, futurescaping even revealed that she had been asking the wrong question, so we repeated the process a second time.

Background

Kat is 67. Divorced with two adult children, she lives in Fulham, London. Her son is a graphic designer and has moved to Rome. Her daughter is married and lives in Manchester. She has two kids of her own and is a solicitor. Kat had a very successful career as a literary agent and co-founded a literary agency, but has recently retired.

Kat owns a big family home that she kept after her divorce. She is considering selling, or perhaps keeping the house and renting it out. Additionally, she is wondering if she does sell, whether she should buy a new place or instead rent out her current home and then rent a smaller house for herself.

Kat is on good terms with her ex-husband who now lives in the United States. She has a core group of friends in London, as well as friends in other parts of the world. She feels that she put a lot of energy into her children and career over the years, and now wants to travel and spend time on herself. She is in good shape physically, values health and looks and feels that both are important to actively maintain.

Kat is not currently in a relationship, but would be open to the possibility of one in the future. Kat has a hunch that there are some parts of the world where after a certain age, it's assumed you don't want a relationship. She feels that to be somewhat true in London, or at least that her current social circle doesn't hold much in terms of romantic prospects.

The house had been an anchor for their family in past years, but it was starting to become a burden for Kat. It was too big for one person, and required pricey and time-consuming upkeep. Kat felt she had an opportunity to explore and enjoy time for herself; something she felt was long overdue.

The question

This is Kat's question as she saw it after our initial discussion:

Should she sell or keep her house and let?

So the sphere is Property Ownership.

Kat thought through all the different ways it could impact her life and we came up with:

Kat's Impact Areas

- Property market
- Children
- Health
- Location
- Social engagement
- Romance
- Travel

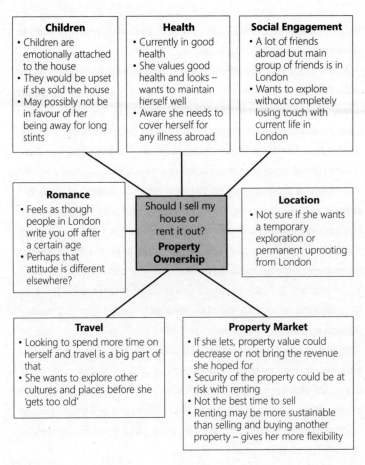

Children
- Children are emotionally attached to the house
- They would be upset if she sold the house
- May possibly not be in favour of her being away for long stints

Health
- Currently in good health
- She values good health and looks – wants to maintain herself well
- Aware she needs to cover herself for any illness abroad

Social Engagement
- A lot of friends abroad but main group of friends is in London
- Wants to explore without completely losing touch with current life in London

Romance
- Feels as though people in London write you off after a certain age
- Perhaps that attitude is different elsewhere?

Should I sell my house or rent it out?
Property Ownership

Location
- Not sure if she wants a temporary exploration or permanent uprooting from London

Travel
- Looking to spend more time on herself and travel is a big part of that
- She wants to explore other cultures and places before she 'gets too old'

Property Market
- If she lets, property value could decrease or not bring the revenue she hoped for
- Security of the property could be at risk with renting
- Not the best time to sell
- Renting may be more sustainable than selling and buying another property – gives her more flexibility

Figure 32

At the beginning of our discussions with Kat, she spoke at length about the current state of the housing market, and her concerns about whether selling or renting her house would be a more sound financial option. House prices were a commonly discussed topic amongst her friends and family, and they were an obvious thing to focus on and worry about. The property market and a generalised anxiety about finances had become her standard excuse for maintaining the status quo and she had wrapped up her life anxiety with falling home values in London.

As we discussed the candidates for her superdriver, however, we realised that although she had first focused on property values when presenting the initial dilemma and this was how she was used to talking about the topic, it did not really concern her. She was, in fact, fairly confident that her house would be easy to sell or let for a good price. She was far more interested in what she would do with the income and was sure that she would like to travel abroad, although she was uncertain how long for. She was open to the idea of permanent relocation, feeling that in many ways it might open new opportunities to 'start a new life' following retirement, with the exciting prospect of new friends and hopefully a new partner. It made sense for this issue of permanent relocation vs extensive travel to be the superdriver and the remaining parameters for her scenarios.

In terms of broader factors, Kat could be facing more difficult cultural attitudes than being seen as old in the dating pool. Some of the more exotic locales she would consider for her retirement could possibly have quite different social and cultural norms in which an older woman living alone could be seen as unusual or inappropriate.

The futurescaping process can be very helpful in making you honest about what is driving you. Kat realised that not only was she fairly confident about property prices, but that even if the financial returns from selling or letting her house were less rosy than she'd hoped for, they still not be the main driver for her decision.

So Kat's x-axis was whether to sell or rent out her house, and her y-axis was permanent relocation vs extensive travel.

Should I sell my house
or rent it out?
Property Ownership

**Permanent
relocation**

PROPERTY MARKET: Selling is slow, but eventually gets a fair, if not ideal, price. Can buy home abroad
CHILDREN: Children strongly dislike this option
HEALTH: Bold move she hopes will be invigorating
LOCATION: This is a huge life change. Might be disorienting at first
SOCIAL ENGAGEMENT: Exciting new chapter with new people to meet
ROMANCE: Might be more opportunities when integrated into a new community
TRAVEL: Fulfils her desires to travel and explore

PROPERTY MARKET: Rent property for steady income, but no lump sum injection of cash. Disposable income quite high
CHILDREN: Children are happy she's keeping the house, but worry about her moving permanently away
HEALTH: Bold move she hopes will be invigorating, but keeping property means keeping old ties
LOCATION: Permanent move, therefore investing in life in new location
SOCIAL ENGAGEMENT: Old friends able to visit if not too far away
ROMANCE: Might be more opportunities when integrated into a new community
TRAVEL: Fulfils her desires to travel and explore, though not as freely with home ownership still a a factor

Sell house ←——————————————————→ **Let house**

PROPERTY MARKET: Selling house gives large lump sum, making her disposable income much higher
CHILDREN: Children still don't like this option, but at least their mother will not be permanently away
HEALTH: Selling house will be a relief and travel she hopes will reinvigorate
LOCATION: Freedom to relocate, but doesn't have to make a decision right away
SOCIAL ENGAGEMENT: Can make new friends travelling and come back to old social circle if she desires
ROMANCE: Might meet someone travelling
TRAVEL: Fulfils her desires to explore and consider places for further travel or relocation

PROPERTY MARKET: Rent property for steady income, but no lump sum injection of cash. Disposable income very high without relocation costs
CHILDREN: Children are most happy with this option, think it is just a phase she needs to get through
HEALTH: Selling house will be a relief and she hopes travel will reinvigorate
LOCATION: Having a lovely time in her travels, but nice to go back to live in London
SOCIAL ENGAGEMENT: Can make new friends travelling and come back to old social circle if she desires
ROMANCE: Could only be a holiday romance
TRAVEL: Fulfils her desires to travel and explore and consider places for further travel

Extensive travel

Figure 33

Initial outcome

Kat's scenarios gave her a picture of what her life might look like if she sold her house or rented it out, if she relocated or just went on an extended holiday. We talked through them, but she didn't seem settled in choosing a preferred or even likely scenario, however. This was not the end of the story.

By thinking through her scenarios, Kat realised that whether or not she ultimately sold her house and relocated, her position on the decision was heavily influenced by her children's feelings. They were very much against her selling their childhood home, despite the fact that neither of them had lived there in years. They wanted a place for their old teddy bears and trophies, and a warm home for family occasions. Kat felt torn: she did not want to upset her kids, but she felt ready to move on. Part of her felt that she shouldn't hold on to the house for the kids' sake, but their happiness was naturally important to her. They had felt even more connected to the house after their parents divorced: it was the last standing reminder of the time when their family had been happy when they were small. The house held a slightly more bittersweet meaning for Kat. It *was* a physical holder of memories of her children, but it also at times reminded her of her divorce and of being alone and sometimes lonely.

Kat thought she was emotionally ready for a reinvention and potentially relocation, but she became aware that her kids' opinions had more importance for her than she had realised. She was, to some degree, using concerns about the housing market as an emotional red herring. It was not, in fact, the property market that was her biggest anxiety. Her house was well sized, attractive and in good condition and it would probably rent or sell easily. However, this allowed her to put a 'respectable' face on her real preoccupation with what her kids might think, not only about the house, but also about what giving it up would say about her as a mother.

She was torn between wanting to assert her independence as a single woman and maintaining her role as mother to her children. This was an especially fraught issue as having retired from a successful job, she was no longer deriving a significant part of her identity from her work. She realised the thing that really mattered to her, rightly or wrongly, was the level of acceptance and approval for her choices from her children.

This realisation led Kat to reframe her question and build a new set of scenarios, with her kids' acceptance of her new life as the variable (y-axis) factor.

Several of the life coaches we spoke to expressed as typical a scenario where someone comes to them for advice and coaching about being successful in their job, only to realise they are in the wrong job. This kind of epiphany echoes what we heard from Kat, who by doing the scenario process, was able to connect with her true feelings on the matter.

Kat reframed her two axes. For her, the real question was whether she should relocate or not in the view of the level of her kids' acceptance. This had been the real question all along. It just took going through the thinking for Kat to really grasp the underlying issues.

Therefore, the x-axis became whether to relocate or travel extensively, in view of the y-axis – the level of acceptance her kids would be able to give her 'reinvention' or new sense of her own life.

This final case study shows the complicated, and somewhat non-rational, factors that are part and parcel of futurescaping for individuals. In this case, we went into a second scenario exercise straight away since the superdriver made itself known through the first set of scenarios.

Should I permanently
relocate or not?
Location

**Kids accept
reinvention**

CHILDREN: Kids visit and maintain ties. Wrench but kids change lives too
SOCIAL ENGAGEMENT: Lonely at first. Support from back home so feels reassured, slowly makes more friends as she is accepted
ROMANCE: Builds permanent relationship
LOCATION: Builds roots and invests in community

CHILDREN: Kids accept the new her and she uses the holidays to reinvigorate her life back at home. She seems more exciting to the children
SOCIAL ENGAGEMENT: She makes friends while travelling
ROMANCE: New friends and possible relationship
LOCATION: Although she stays in London, she works harder to find interesting new hobbies and friends

**Permanent
relocation** ←——————————→ **Extensive
travel**

CHILDREN: Kids feel abandoned. Tense family relations.
Children make it hard to see the grandchildren. Kids feel betrayed. Still seen as a rebellious act. Just a phase.
Betrayed by father and mother
SOCIAL ENGAGEMENT: She puts more time and effort into making new friends, although she feels a hole from lack of family contact
ROMANCE: Puts effort into dating and finding new relationships
LOCATION: Builds roots and invests in new community

CHILDREN: Kids are bemused. She tries to prove herself to kids – goes for more crazy locations. Could be dangerous
SOCIAL ENGAEMENT: May be perceived as a delayed midlife crisis. Lonely – hasn't found a group of friends yet. Sometimes feels like she's replicating teenage lifestyle
ROMANCE: Has made a few friends, but no lasting relationships
LOCATION: Feels a bit in-between. Not getting support in London, but not anywhere else long enough to build support system

Kids don't accept reinvention

Figure 34

The final outcome

Once Kat had drilled down to her real feelings and biases regarding the house decision and relocation, she was able to form a more rational case to discuss with her kids. Her kids were mature enough to handle a discussion regarding the house (she hoped!). They also wanted her to be happy, although they may be uncomfortable with the amount of change she was proposing.

The futurescaping process was useful for Kat because she was able to really understand what her question was – and what it wasn't.

Kat's view

'Your process was the best thing I could have done! It's helped me sort out a huge emotional mess. It's quite funny as I consider myself to be cool-headed and rational. I realised I am far more influenced by what my kids and friends think than I thought or might have liked. I do seek their approval whether I like it or not. I need to understand for myself if talking about something as drastic as relocation is a rebellion or some sort of midlife crisis, but I'm now very clear that I want to move on.

'I will not just make a rash decision or drop this like a bomb on my kids, but it no longer makes sense for me to make every decision as a mother, which I have done for years.'

So...

So, hopefully now you are more than comfortable with the futurescaping process. If you haven't already, I would obviously encourage you to give it a go. You don't have to do it all from A to Z straight off. And once you get comfortable with this process, there is no reason why you can't play with it a little.

As you have seen through the case studies, futurescaping is a way in to planning, on seeing your future as a story so you can get objective enough to see the best way forward. It's a way to approach something that is so daunting to so many, at least in their personal lives.

If you do feel ready to give it a try, then pick a decision you are facing, and think why it matters. If you can see how you decide having a serious impact on your life in five years' time, then go through and think about all the areas which it might affect. The Appendix has the general list of 'life spheres' that your decision is likely to fall into with some suggested impact areas to get you started on thinking through what broader issues are influencing – or will be influenced by – the decision.

Look through what you've got down so far, draw your x-axis and label it with the decision, and then on to identifying the superdriver. Once that's done, there's your y-axis, and four inviting boxes waiting for you to imagine how your future life might turn out in four different ways.

Where you do it

A final note on methodology. All of the people we got to run through the futurescaping process confirmed that a change of scenery was helpful in helping them change their state of mind about the future. So best to try to think about career options away from your desk, or house buying away from your cramped flat.

Gaining some physical space from the question at hand might help you gain some useful mental distance as well.

With any luck (not that we believe in that sort of thing), you'll be able to construct some likely scenarios which will help you think through the kinds of decisions you'll need to make to get to your preferable scenario – a satisfying and successful future as defined by you.

Next up, we're going to discuss what to do after you've finished your futurescaping.

9

Driving Back from the Future and Early Warnings

'In my next life, I want to live my life backwards. You start out dead and get that out of the way. Then you wake up in an old people's home feeling better every day. You get kicked out for being too healthy, go collect your pension, and then when you start work, you get a gold watch and a party on your first day. You work for 40 years until you're young enough to enjoy your retirement. You party, drink alcohol, and are generally promiscuous, then you are ready for high school. You then go to primary school, you become a kid, you play. You have no responsibilities, you become a baby until you are born. And then you spend your last nine months floating in luxurious spa-like conditions with central heating and room service on tap, larger quarters every day and then Voilà! You finish off as an orgasm!'

– Woody Allen (slightly different version also attributed to George Carlin)

Happily ever after...

So hopefully you've had a go at futurescaping and decided the best way forward on your decision. You're now left with two scenarios, above and below the x-axis. The process should have already proved its usefulness, but there is more to come.

Full scenario planning is an immersive and often exhausting experience. The process to frame the question, identify and analyse the drivers, and then create the scenarios requires participants to really be open and think deeply and in new ways. Depending on the aims decided at the outset, it is possible that the aims are fulfilled once the scenarios are complete and it could all end there. For example, in the case of corporate scenario planning, the aims may simply be limited to getting a group of people to share and exchange ideas and create stronger bonds between team members: intellectual team building. In this case, the scenarios could almost be seen as a bonus coming out of the exercise. The team will have built something which can be far more useful to themselves and the organisation than some raft made out of sticks and cling film, or the bruises of paintballing.

Sometimes companies want to use the scenarios as PR collateral, proving to the world that they have been creatively thinking ahead. So they publish them with fanfare and nice graphics. In the process outlined in the previous chapter, the initial aim is fulfilled once you have been able to decide one way or the other. However, the usefulness of the scenarios and the process can and should go well beyond that.

Once the scenarios have been painted there are many ways to build further and use them to develop strategy. As Peter Schwartz says, 'looking into the future is most useful when it is the beginning, not the end, of a significant conversation'[89]. People have a strong tendency to pick their favourite scenario – 'I'll have that future, please'. This is usually frowned upon, as the world just doesn't work that way. However, there is nothing wrong with expressing the appeal of one outcome over another. If there is

---

89   Schwartz, Peter. *The Art of the Long View*. Hoboken, New Jersey: Wiley, 1997.

something within one's locus of control which can hasten or put off the development of any of the scenarios then it should be identified and deployed.

Scenarios in and of themselves may be useful as warning bells, forcing an otherwise apathetic audience to understand that a nightmare scenario could conceivably and logically emerge from existing and apparent drivers. After all, Herman Kahn, the pioneer of scenario planning, forced people to really sit up and think about the prospect of thermonuclear war by painting a scenario of what the world would be like *following* such a war.

Developing goals and strategies

There is a lot of evidence to suggest that having a sense of desirable future outcomes, of a goal that you work back from, can allow you to forge a path to get there. Similarly, you can also emerge with a sense of likely obstacles and outcomes to avoid. As Katerina Gould, executive coach, sees it, 'once you have thought about it and other avenues also, you can proceed with more confidence because you know it is the right thing. You have a bigger perspective, and are likely to be more successful at it, and have worked out who else you need to involve'[90].

All of the life coaches we spoke to highlighted the importance of tangible goals to create personal strategy. Several mentioned the usefulness of the SMART acronym. This means making sure that any goal you have is Specific, Measurable, Attainable, Relevant and Timely. The common good sense becomes even more obvious if you look at what the inverse would mean: goals which are Vague, Unmeasurable, Unattainable, Irrelevant and Untimely. VUUIU clearly doesn't make any sense at all, not like being SMART.

---

90   In conversation with the author.

Once the scenarios have been developed, there are two basic ways in which they can then go on to be used:

1. develop strategies for each of the scenarios;

2. develop an early warning system so that you can be aware as soon as possible when the world moves in the direction of one of the scenarios.

Strategies and Early Warning Systems

No one is suggesting that the future is going to look exactly like one of the scenarios. Rather, what usually happens is that the future is an amalgamation of all of the scenarios. Whatever the question, whatever the outcome, building the scenarios will have exposed your thinking to new vulnerabilities and opportunities. By anticipating obstacles you have a better chance of overcoming them. One thing you could do is look at the scenarios and do a SWOT analysis for each one: what are your strengths and weaknesses, opportunities and threats in that future world? What can you do now to optimise your strengths and opportunities or limit your weaknesses and vulnerability to threats?

Let's look at how doing the process has been useful for our case studies. For Tom, vacillating between applying for management consultancy or the US State Department, the nexus of his scenario process was the tension between intellectual fulfilment and financial reward and status. In terms of early warning, he is now forewarned and therefore forearmed against the possibility that, having chosen consultancy, his work/life balance may become seriously compromised, and has set himself a number of non-work goals (e.g. running a marathon next year) which he will take as a proxy sign for whether or not he is maintaining the right balance or heading towards midlife burnout and loneliness. Conversely, he has a clear sense of what success looks like in consultancy, attainment of a certain grade with a certain salary within five years, and will be using that to assess whether his status/financial goals are being met. He will get a sense fairly swiftly as to whether he is a rising star of the firm or not climbing quickly enough. He also identified that he will be fulfilled by the intellectual rewards of becoming more specialised, so he has drawn up a career strategy to try to bring that forward.

Duncan, who decided he was going to buy a house in Aberdeen, realised how much his livelihood is dependent on popular taste. If taste for nostalgia declines, he will need to retrain so that he can find work beyond his current niche. He decided he would proactively keep a watching brief on how popular taste for nostalgia was developing, rather than just relying on a sense of how much business there is around. Keeping track of changing tastes by going to visit furniture departments in stores (going on 'retail safari', if any of his friends ask), watching home renovation shows on TV, flicking through interior design magazines, keeping an eye out for hotel design, not always skipping the magazine section on men's fashion as he normally does, Duncan will be able to develop an early warning system for his business pipeline. Tracking the trendsetters in associated related areas will give him a bit of a 'heads up' on changing fashions, and time to respond effectively.

On the strategic front, he is starting to consider possibilities for how his mum might best be cared for in future years. Can her house be adapted? Can he help her with any financial planning? He is also going to analyse the costs, tax issues and risks of taking on a lodger. This looked to be a no-regret move for both scenarios he had created, providing some level of companionship and an extra injection of financial stability.

John, torn between carrying on in a boring job or starting his own business, realised he was able to hedge his bets, setting up something small before he takes the plunge. By going through the process, he realised how risk-averse his personality is. He decided to move slowly, starting up the business on the side whilst continuing in his current job. This way, he will get some early warnings, in so far as he can see whether he can get any customers, whether he has the stomach for selling or the mindset to run a business, whilst maintaining connections in his old job. He agreed to move beyond his starry-eyed desire to be an entrepreneur, somehow magically free from his current rut, and write a business plan. He will also explore with his partner exactly how they would be affected in terms of his changed financial circumstances if he were to leave his job, rather than relying on a vague assumption that it would all be fine.

It ain't over

Scenario planning is not meant to be something you do only once. Like all future planning, as we change and the world around us changes, we need to keep looking, keep readjusting our assumptions and calculations, keep recalibrating or reinventing our future plans. How soon do scenarios go stale? Well they definitely have a half life, beyond which not only do they become less meaningful and less useful, but as time progresses the connection that you have with the process, how it opened your mind, how you felt, what you learned, becomes weaker, so they pack a less powerful rational and emotional punch.

It's difficult to set a definitive perfect frequency, but an annual appraisal, at least, sounds about right. It depends how much capacity you have for change and tweaking. As Mike Roberts says: 'We review our plan to win three times a year: a sense of where we're taking the business, checking if it is it still applicable and what disruptors are emerging. We're monitoring developments. I made a decision that we would have china in our LYFE restaurants, but our customers can't put a knife and fork down without having it slide around in a circle. It's got to be a continuous improvement journey. We'll modify the shape of the china. And yet I thought long and hard about the china, our testers loved it. I learned something'[91].

We should keep planning for the future as we change. Our goals and values shift. As Carol Rosati pointed out: 'What you wanted in your twenties is not what you want in your forties. Quite often people think being a CFO of a FTSE 100 is the be-all and end-all, but then they get there and they don't like the view anymore.'[92]

So beyond the decision and beyond the scenarios, having a go at this process, and repeating it, will have an overall beneficial impact on how you manage your future, and therefore how you view the world. Doing this process will impact you in many positive ways, all of which will contribute to raising your Future Quotient.

What are the benefits beyond making the basic decision? Increasing your FQ

- **Broadening your perspective,** using your imagination, releasing creativity about what matters to you most to open up your eyes to new possibilities.
- **Getting the 'objective habit',** repeated efforts to analyse and distil your challenges will enhance your ability to disengage from the emotional clutter and respond rationally.
- **Becoming more self-aware,** seeing yourself from the outside will allow you a new understanding of what drives you, what matters to you, and how you operate.

---

91 In conversation with the author.
92 Ibid.

- **Knowing your place** in the best way, having a sense of where you fit in your world and what you can and can't control.
- **Filtering information more smartly and effectively,** knowing what factors you need to look out for and be aware of, what you can and can't control.
- **Future fluency and systems fluency** helps you understand how things interconnect, building the ability to think forward and work out the steps you need to take to get somewhere you want to go.
- **Limiting fear and managing uncertainty** helps you to worry the right amount.

Conclusion

'If we omitted all that is unclear, we would probably be left completely uninteresting and trivial tautologies.'
Werner Heisenberg

So, we have reached the end. This is the point when I could say that now you know all you will ever need to know. Now that the mystery has been revealed and the magic baton passed, you can go forth, make better decisions, plan your future and sort your life out. But while it is tempting for me to believe that – and maybe tempting for you now you've bought and hopefully read the book – it would be wrong to suggest that there is anything magic or mystical here, any shred of transcendental wisdom. (If you have only just realised this, then perhaps I can suggest a more thorough re-read, particularly of Chapters 1 to 9.)

Futurescaping is simply about advocating an open and rational attitude to future planning, and taking a technique from business and applying it with the kind of objective mindset which we can all deploy at work but somehow are less able to do at home.

Important decisions *should* take time. Evolutionary biology may explain how our brains are shaped for quick decisions to fight or flee from beasts, but such decision-making is less useful for comparing APRs and mpg and thinking about where a transformational decision in career or home might take us.

The future remains uncertain. We are surrounded by flux and change and it can be tempting to simply keep our eyes down and find only what is immediately around us as urgent or important. But when we find the courage and the curiosity and allow ourselves the time to look up, we can discern patterns in the chaos. We should try to create the most realistic and rational pattern possible, borrowing and learning from wherever or whatever might help us, so that when it comes to something as important as understanding our own lives, we can best create what we want from the reality of our futures. The pattern we discern will always be a story, a representation of reality which we tell ourselves.

Stories are important. I don't mean fantasies here, or the kind of stories which deliberately distort, but story in the sense of trying to find a bridge of reason between cause and effect, some kind of logic created to cover what would otherwise just be a gap. This is the right way to go. Just because something contains an element of uncertainty does not mean we should ignore any attempt at logic, at trying to make sense of what is going on and what is likely to happen.

It won't be perfect, it won't be accurate, but at least you will be better prepared. It's not about being right, it's about being ready.

Appendix

Life Sphere:	Potential impact areas:

Career
- Intellectual and personal fulfilment
- Salary expectations and financial standing
- Progress, status and recognition
- Job market/job security and stability
- Permanent employment vs freelance vs entrepreneurship
- Work/life balance
- Location and commute
- Ethics and social responsibility
- Ability to travel with work
- Leisure time/time for hobbies
- Ability to maintain social life
- Ability to see family/relatives
- Ability to maintain/forge new romantic relationships
- Opportunities for new friends
- Benefits/perks of the company e.g. insurance, pension, free gym membership, discounts and subscriptions
- Holiday allowances and flexibility

Pet ownership
- Emotional fulfilment
- Type of pet and suitable breed for your lifestyle
- Finances – pet insurance, kennelling, vet bills, pet food

- Personal health – pets may improve health with added physical exercise
- Ability to maintain social life
- Ability to travel and spend time away from home
- Family/partner – allergies? Appropriate pet for children?
- Environment – e.g. small flat, no access to outdoor space
- Career – long hours and extensive business trips not conducive to pet ownership

---

Having children

- Health
- Career
- Ability to travel/mobility
- Time
- Finances
- Quality of local education
- Wider family attitude/support
- Religious issues
- Size of house
- Need for mother's help/childcare – au pair, nanny, babysitting
- Environment and ethics
- The needs of any current children
- The needs of any other dependants

Child's education

- Family finances
- Long-term financial commitment
- Ability to travel

- Quality of local education
- Alignment between family's political or social outlook and school's
- Community angle
- Ethics of state/private education

Elective surgery

- Emotional impact
- Surgical risks
- Career relevance
- Finances
- Health and physical mobility immediately after and long-term
- Care of dependants
- Hobbies and lifestyle
- Time out of work/lost wages

Location

- Abroad or in home country
- Commuting expenditure
- Ability to maintain social life and leisure activities
- Ability to see family/relatives
- Healthcare availability and quality
- Community
- Near to necessary amenities – schools, hospitals, place of work, gym etc.
- Environment and lifestyle – urban, suburban, rural

Property	<ul><li>Rent or buy?</li><li>Increased or decreased sense of rootedness to community (long-term or short-term)?</li><li>Finances related to investment and housing market</li><li>Home maintenance – investment of time and money</li><li>Ability to maintain or improve social life or romantic relationships</li><li>Alter social habits e.g. if buying a house you may be more inclined to socialise at home</li><li>Lifestyle for your dependants, children and pets</li><li>Ability to travel or be away</li><li>Child's schooling</li><li>Emotional impact</li><li>Feeling of security vs feeling of entrapment</li></ul>
Financial investments	<ul><li>Risk – are these investments relatively certain or speculative?</li><li>Broader economic regional, national, or international climate</li><li>Tax</li><li>Long-term benefits – financial return, possible retirement fund or inheritance for children</li><li>Opportunity cost while money tied up/ease of exit</li></ul>

	• Quality and cost of advice
	• Monitoring required?
	• Potential impact negative result could have on you or family

Living together	• Emotion – sense of rootedness and stability versus giving up independence and alone time
	• Location (and life areas associated with it, see above)
	• Finances – sharing living costs
	• Social norms or family expectations
	• Progression of relationship

Have relationship	• Emotional fulfilment etc.
	• Sense of connectedness and support
	• Career and work/life balance
	• Independence and reduced personal time
	• Relationships with friends or family
	• Social norms or family expectations
	• Children

Index